A THERAPIST'S NOTEBOOK
Day-to-Day Notes of a Psychotherapist

BOB GOODKIN, Ph.D.
Montclair State College and
Private Practice

LENOX BOOKS

Copyright © 1981 by
Bob Goodkin

Library of Congress Catalog Card
Number 81-90025

International Standard Book Number 0-9605872-0-9

Printed in the United States of America

Published by
LENOX BOOKS
P.O. Box 104
Little Falls, New Jersey 07424

TO MY LOVE, DIANE

CONTENTS

Introduction	3
Notes	6
Some Patients	89
A Final Note	115
Some Books	117

My intention in this notebook is to include-primarily in brief entries-impressions, thoughts, and feelings relating to myself and my work as a psychologist. Although there are many books and articles on the theory and the practice of psychotherapy, I do not find many honest, real, personal writings in this very personal, human area, and I've always enjoyed hearing and reading about such things.

I guess I'm writing this book for me, other psychotherapists, students of psychology, people in therapy, and anyone else interested in the day-to-day work and existence of a psychologist who has spent considerable time doing psychotherapy, psychological research involving people with problems, and teaching psychology. To me, it's interesting to consider who a writer is talking to. Sometimes, it seems that the writer is talking to some vague abstraction out there. Often, writing in this area comes across as a very impersonal, intellectualized statement of some subject matter on one's mind. Many times writers just seem to be verbally masturbating to impress themselves or others with their knowledge or insights. I'm hoping to write something real for me and you, something relating to real life among people. In the process, I hope to learn something, to share some experiences from what I feel is a most fascinating, personally rewarding, and enriching way of life, and if I make a few bucks in the process, that would be O.K., too. Since I do not view this as a technical or heavy theoretical book, I will do my best to write it in English.

In a nutshell, I'm now 43 years old, and have had a Ph.D. in my field since I was 26. After working as a research assistant and school psychologist while in graduate school, I served a clinical internship at NYU Medical Center, remained in that setting as a Research Associate and Senior Research Psychologist working with physically disabled children and adults, taught undergraduate and graduate courses in two colleges, worked as a consultant to state agencies involved with children and disabled people, and have had a general private practice in psychology for the past fourteen years. I've written quite a few papers, articles, and chapters relating mainly to my work at the medical center. I've been married to Diane for 20 years and have two children, David, 17, and Janet, 15.

In this book I discuss mainly what I do in my work and my honest reactions, thoughts and feelings about it. I'm not doing this because I see myself as such a brilliant example of what a therapist should be or as having revolutionary, innovative ideas about the treatment of human woes. The thought is more that much of what I have read has little relationship with what real, honest-to-goodness, day-to-day psychotherapy is about, and writers often leave themselves out, when this is such a vital part of the business. My experience as a therapist, and discussing work with other therapists, leads me to believe that the daily practice of psychotherapy is generally quite different from the way most books discuss psychotherapy. So many writers seem to set up and knock down straw men in order to support their particular theories and approaches.

Some of the notes deal with basic, elemental, human concepts in as unembarrassed a way as possible. Books on therapy often don't devote much space to such topics as honesty, caring, and putting yourself in the place of the patient, for example. Perhaps this is because such factors are assumed or it is hoped that readers will pick these things up between the lines. I feel, however, that these issues are at least as important as any others in the practice of therapy, and I run into many practicing therapists who are seriously lacking in these areas.

Personal experiences from childhood, growing up, and the present, relate to the kind of person the therapist is and to the way he functions in therapy. I include some discussions of personal experiences to give an idea of how such events relate to my understanding of my own life and work, sometimes directly, sometimes indirectly. A therapist can learn a great deal from all kinds of experiences that will be helpful in understanding, relating to, and doing something about his patient's behavior. He can find inspiration and relevant ideas in many areas that may initially appear to have little in common with his work. I often feel that such experiences have as much to teach me as teachers and books on psychotherapy.

I will discuss people, therapy, how some events in my life relate to my work, and things that have helped me in my efforts to understand and change unwanted feelings and behavior. Although the book touches upon theory, the emphasis is on the day-to-day practice of psychotherapy.

Although discussions of people I have worked with in therapy are taken from actual cases, I changed the names and other identifying information to assure their privacy.

NOTES

Just as A.S. Neill stressed that the school should be made to fit the child rather than having the child fit the school, I feel that therapy should be geared to fit the individual patient, rather than making the patient fit the therapy.

* * * * *

I know this sounds terribly unscientific, but the more I learn about and experience the field of psychotherapy the more I feel that what the individual therapist *is* rings louder than what he or she *does*. His intelligence, sensitivity, genuine caring, values, creativity, and ability to see through bullshit (the patients and his own) are more important than his techniques, theories, and procedures-although these are certainly very important, too.

* * * * *

Although I am generally identified as a behavior therapist, on the basis of the orientation of my graduate school, my research, writings, and courses taught, I have found that in having a private practice, not everyone coming for therapy is treated best with this approach. While an understanding of learning theory and learning concepts is very valuable in understanding and dealing with many situations, the needs of many people coming for therapy are often not best treated by behavior therapy procedures. Unless one establishes a practice devoted to a very specific specialty such as dealing with overweight people, smokers, phobic behavior, etc., it is necessary to be open to hearing many kinds of problems and to using a variety of approaches. The aim is to be open to the person, try to determine the person's needs, consider whether you can work with the person and meet his or her particular needs. If one has a general practice in psychotherapy, being a narrow cultist would certainly not meet the needs of many individuals coming for therapy. Some of the people coming to you just need a safe place to ventilate or scream their guts out, some need to conceptualize their situations differently, some need understanding and approval, some have to be hit over the head with how they are lying to themselves, some need specific advice, some need a concrete program for making specific changes, and so forth.

* * * * *

For years theorists in the field of psychology got far on such factors as eloquence and personal charisma. As in other fields, people hop on bandwagons. Many psychotherapists are pretty good with words, partly I guess, because they spend so much time sitting and talking. Even Freud was nominated for a Nobel Prize in literature, rather than science or medicine (not to minimize his monumental contribution to therapy). One healthy influence of behaviorism, and experimental psychology in general, is the stress on stating theories in a testable way. Early theorists introduced many appealing concepts which were not measurable in terms of behavior. The main trouble with this was that after a while hundreds of "reasonable" concepts relating to behavior and therapy (some very contradictory) existed side by side. You pays your money and you takes your choice. Many theorists spoke knowledgably and impressively about mythology, history, and religion, for example, leaving the reader with a sense of "Wow, this guy's smart. Alot of what he says makes sense. Who am I to question him?" But, internalizing concepts, without evidence or without carefully filtering them through our own brains is not generally a good practice. I feel it's healthier to read ideas with a spirit of "Yes, this makes sense to me. No, that doesn't. There is good evidence for this. That sounds good, but is there any evidence to support it?"

* * * * *

I was really never crazy about the term 'eclectic' because in my head it was generally associated with mushy thinking. I felt that because someone did not or could not think through an area to the degree of committing himself to a solid model, he took a little here and a little there without fully understanding any area. We all see some people who get very excited about each new popular technique or theory that comes along. At the opposite end of this continuum is the person who is not open to any new point of view. For me, the most desirable approach is to be open to new ideas, and if they make sense to you, work hard to really learn them well in order that you can draw upon them when the situation calls for it. I have some strong preferences regarding theories and procedures in psychotherapy, and there are some that I don't like at all. I try to learn, understand, and get a feel for those theories and procedures that I believe will help me in my work and in my life. If that makes me eclectic, then I guess I'm eclectic.

* * * * *

Psychotherapy is an extremely complex business. It includes the art, science, and underlying philosophy of what you are doing. The art, as I see it, includes such areas as establishing a relationship with the individual or individuals, being sensitive to the person's needs, words, motor behavior, voice quality, facial expressions, etc. One's sensitivity toward and awareness of one's own feelings and thoughts, the feelings and thoughts of the other, and the ongoing situations of both are very important areas in what I view as the art of therapy. Many factors are constantly changing and are difficult to isolate and quantify. It is also frequently very difficult to identify what behaviors to focus on and what the desired behavior changes might be. Sometimes the indicated desired changes are clear, but much more often they are subtle and not very clear at all. It is a very real and difficult issue to determine, with the patient, what behaviors (motor, verbal, emotional, attitudinal) should be changed to what. A constant sensitivity to the individual, and to his situation, thoughts, emotions, attitudes, is a very important part of the ongoing sessions, and this aspect of therapy, at least at this time, is more related to the art than to the science of psychotherapy.

The science aspect of therapy concerns the idea that there are basic principles of behavior which have been carefully researched, and which aid in understanding and offer real leverage in bringing about changes in behavior (motor, emotional, verbal, social, attitudinal.) There is already a great deal of evidence to suggest that behavior is a legitimate area of scientific study, and that the prediction and control of specific behaviors is very possible. The effects of such behavioral learning principles as reinforcement, extinction, punishment, and modeling, for example, have been proven in many arenas with many species and a wide variety of behaviors. To deny the scientific and technological findings of psychology is to close one's eyes to a great amount of convincing evidence.

Concerning the underlying philosophy of what one is doing in psychotherapy involves defining what one wishes to accomplish as well as what he believes he is doing. There are many schools of thought in psychotherapy. Some are very concerned about changing specific behaviors; some attempt to help a patient understand himself better, believing that this understanding will automatically lead to meaningful changes; some feel the therapist directs the changes; some feel that the job of the therapist is to provide an atmosphere for growth and change; some focus on techniques based on learning principles; some focus on interpreting and providing insights on unconscious motives. Of course, many things are occurring beyond the awareness of the therapist. The actual effective or ineffective ingredients of therapy might be very different from those described by the therapist. The effects of ongoing sessions are frequently experienced by the patient as being much more or much less effective than I believe them to be.

While different therapists experience the intent and process of therapy very differently, I feel that all three aspects-the art, science, and underlying philosophy of therapy-are important and relevant elements to consider. The daily practice of therapy often calls for an understanding of and respect for contributions from both humanism and science.

* * * * *

What the therapist and patient say was done and experienced in a therapy session frequently differs in some ways. And, a recording of the session often gives the listener still another impression of what transpired. The therapist and patient can *experience* the same session quite differently, and what one *says* about it is frequently limited or altered by many factors-such as the focus (selective attention) and awareness of each at the time, defenses, memory, or concern about giving the listener a particular impression.

* * * * *

In practicing psychotherapy, it is not realistic to use just one theoretical model or approach unless you have a very specialized practice. If someone is coming to you because of a fear of speaking in groups or of flying in planes, it is usually kind of silly to spend alot of time analyzing the hell out of the person's past experiences, dreams, fantasies, etc. unless the person wants to spend time and money in such activities. I find that in such cases a behavior therapy approach is much faster, more direct, and in line with the individual's wants and needs. On the other hand, if the person comes to therapy to explore himself and his motivations, etc., it would be wrong to attempt to con this individual into some narrowly focused behavior change model. In so many books dealing with therapy, the authors come across as if their new way is the best way, the answer, the right way to deal with people who enter psychotherapy. If the author has something to teach me that will help me to work better with some people, terrific. But, people come to therapy with too many different kinds of problems and needs to fit into a single, narrow model.

* * * * *

Having worked as a psychologist in a variety of institutional settings (hospitals, colleges, etc.), one of the most enjoyable aspects of a private practice for me is the relative absence of politics. You are primarily responsible to the patient and yourself, and you don't have to worry too much about what administrators, people in superior positions, or colleagues feel you should do, or about frequently justifying your actions to them. For me, this has been a more conducive atmosphere for putting all of my energies into the sessions. I've found that even in the most tolerant, understanding, supportive institutional positions, escaping from institutional and social pressures (overt or subtle) is impossible. I see some people who seem to love power games in these settings, but I don't. This is not to say that having a private practice is all joy. I generally don't get much pleasure writing reports or administering lengthy tests, for example, but the relative absence of the political pressures experienced in other settings is a definite benefit of private practice for me.

* * * * *

A therapist has to be capable of functioning with flexibility and a degree of ambiguity in his work. It generally takes some time to understand what a patient really needs and to come up with a treatment approach that will be meaningful and effective. In this field it often takes time for things to fall into place for both the therapist and the patient. If constantly being on top of it and knowing exactly what you are doing each step of the way is very important to you, you would probably be happier as a draftsman, mechanic, dentist, etc. than as a psychotherapist. Although these vocations also certainly have areas of ambiguity and confusion, the factors to be considered and worked with are generally more concise and limited than those of a therapist, and people in these fields often get faster and more concrete feedback on the results of their work. In therapy, while it is desirable to objectively assess procedures and progress in the areas being treated, one often has to be willing to work for some time before he can really see the effects of his labors. Therapy requires a great deal of patience and tolerance for ambiguity.

* * * * *

I often like a degree of chaos in the air while I'm working in therapy or teaching. It reassures me that what we're doing is linked with the real world. When things are moving along too smoothly, I'm suspicious that maybe what we're doing is not for real.

* * * * *

What you do in therapy has to be tailored to the needs of the individual. Having a general practice in the suburbs such as mine, I find every kind of person under the sun coming in-children, adults; little problems, big problems; real problems, self-imposed problems. There's just no single way to deal with these many varied situations. It's not easy to be a wise man.

* * * * *

Everyone comes to you with some expectations as to what therapy is all about. These expectations can range from being very close to your way of operating to miles apart from it. During the first few sessions you find out, among other things, how the early experiencing of therapy relates to his expectations. You don't want to blend into the person's expectations and you don't want to mold the person into doing it your way. You work out what "the way" will be together, and "the way" might change as you go along.

* * * * *

I think it's a good idea for a therapist to be open to many ideas about therapy. I see so many people put down any kind of therapy that doesn't feel comfortable to them immediately, and I feel that this is wrong. "This therapy is too superficial and mechanistic", "That therapy is too spooky and mystical." Often, anything unfamiliar doesn't feel right at first. You have to study it, try to feel it, learn about the philosophy behind it, and study the procedures and outcome data.

* * * * *

In his book, *Zen and the Art of Motorcycle Maintenance,* Robert Pirsig discussed the philosophical differences between classical and romantic understanding. While classical understanding stresses the underlying form or structure of things, romantic understanding focuses more on immediate appearance. Relating this distinction to motorcycles, for example, he explained that a person who sees the machine primarily from a classical viewpoint would be interested in its parts and their functional relationships; the individual with a romantic viewpoint would be mainly interested in the beauty of the motorcycle, its excitement, and the feeling it gives him. A person with the classical orientation may have very little interest in the romantic point of view, and visa versa. I find this to be an interesting way to look at behavior and the process of therapy. One can view behavior mainly in its more wholistic, "big picture", molar, *romantic* form, or one might be more attuned to the underlying processes that account for the behavior-that is, to the *classical* understanding of behavior. Relating this idea to the process of therapy, some therapists focus more on larger aspects of behavior, while others are more concerned with the underlying form, such as principles of behavior or of personality. I believe that in viewing both behavior and the process of therapy, it is entirely possible to appreciate and use both classical and romantic understanding, although at a given time one may be more or less tuned into one side. I don't think it has to be an either/or choice.

* * * * *

I like the emphasis on the importance of "the relationship" in therapy sessions. Regardless of your procedures and theory, if you don't establish a meaningful relationship with the person you're dealing with, forget it. Sometimes there are such differences in your backgrounds or personalities that there appears to be no way in which you can develop a good rapport. If this is so, it is unlikely that you will be useful to this person. When I left graduate school and was convinced that a very "scientific", behavioristic approach to dealing with problems was "the way", I lost some patients early in the game because I was coming across too machine-like. If you are not responding to the person in front of you with his immediate concerns, feelings, and thoughts, you will soon lose him regardless of the adequacy of your theoretical framework or procedures. Working with people in psychotherapy has taught me that how you come across as a person is very important in making contact with the individual, gaining his trust, and helping him to change.

* * * * *

Thoreau's observation that "the majority of men lead lives of quiet desperation" is certainly as true today as it was in his day. As a therapist, one soon sees that under the surface, most people carry around many insecurities, depressing thoughts, and aspects of their lives and behavior that they would like to change. Many times in my college classes, I have done a brief exercise where I ask students to write a "secret" or something about themselves that they are concerned about which they were unlikely to reveal to others, even people they felt quite close to. Invariably, everyone in the class writes something. A great variety of things are written-frequently concerning subjects such as wishing for a close friend, uncomfortable feelings in interpersonal situations, guilt about sexual feelings, discontent with a family member, or anxiety or fear in some area. Of course, people try to cover up these feelings with all sorts of surface behaviors. Laing, the Scottish psychiatrist, suggests that often highly anxious people don't appear anxious at all, because they put so much energy into covering up these feelings, from others and themselves. Every day we encounter people who talk about sports, business, politics, and so forth in an effort to avoid revealing themselves and where they are really living to others.

* * * * *

After seeing patients with very great, real problem situations like Steven and Jennifer or like Lois, it is sometimes frustrating, by contrast, to work with some others whose depression or anxiety is so much more self-imposed. A half year ago, Steven, age 9, and Jennifer, 8, saw their alcoholic father shoot and kill their mother and grandmother, whom they were very attached to. They are now living with an aunt and uncle, and although they have been very active and had some bad nightmares since the incident, they have been adjusting remarkably well to their new home and new school.

How does one begin to adjust to such an experience? Lois, a 35 year old divorced woman, has recently lost the use of her legs from a progressive neuro-muscular disease. She has four children, the youngest of whom is severely autistic and the oldest is neurologically impaired. She had (and still periodically fights) a drug addiction problem which started when she was prescribed certain drugs to cope better with her back pain. She also has very little money, and a variety of other reality problems. Although she sometimes has difficulty in coping (who wouldn't?), she meets her responsibilities head on and stays more or less on top of them.

Many of the people I've worked with in therapy had far less in the way of real problem situations in their lives but felt much more overwhelmed with anxiety and depression. It doesn't generally help, in a long-term way, to tell these people how unfortunate other individuals are-they know there are others who have it worse. To each person, his own problems are real, and are certainly the most important ones, to him.

* * * * *

With many individuals who come for psychotherapy, I get the impression that what they are looking for more than anything else is someone who really cares about them. Many people feel very much alone and even with many acquaintances feel that what they do or how they feel makes little real difference to anyone.

* * * * *

It is not easy to be a caring-machine. If one really doesn't care about the lives of people, I question whether he or she could be an effective therapist. I think such feelings are often sensed quite soon by patients, just as genuine feelings of caring are generally sensed. Some patients pretend that they do not feel the therapist really gives a damn out of a need to manipulate the therapist (e.g. to get the therapist to express caring more). Some people seem to have a nearly bottomless pit of a need to hear expressions of caring. Often these people come from homes where they have received very little real caring from their parents when they were young. You generally have to be very patient with these people because it may take a long time before they will be convinced that anyone really does care. Another aspect of dealing with such people is to point out this need to them directly as you see it, to reflect to them how they might turn people away or don't allow them to care. Showing a person his behavior very honestly and directly as you sense it is, I feel, a very essential part of therapy.

Naturally, there are times when it is very difficult to express caring. If the therapist has been working long hours or is preoccupied with other events in his life, it has to carry over into the session to some degree. I have found my own attitude toward a day in which I have many patients scheduled (say 8 or more) to vary. Some days I welcome it, other days I just jump in and do the best I can although I do not welcome it at all. Perhaps some people can be very involved and caring with every patient even if they see 8 or more a day, 5 or 6 days a week, but it's very hard for me to conceive of it. At times, being a psychotherapist seems to be such an unnatural vocation-spending so many hours a day dealing with people's most upsetting problems. As a rule, I prefer to see a varied caseload (kids, young adults, older adults, elderly people) of about 5 or 6 people a day and to break the therapy hours up with other activities in other settings during the day. I don't feel I'm of much good to the people I see if I'm not feeling alive and interested.

* * * * *

I started this book a few months ago. After a couple of years of not doing much research or writing, I thought I would spend some time on a book which I've long felt an urge to work on. I haven't written a damn thing in weeks. Diane and I are now on vacation in the Berkshires in Massachusetts. I'm sitting on a blanket in Tanglewood (summer home of the Boston Symphony Orchestra), sketching and listening to Brahms' First Symphony, Ozawa conducting. We've had a fantastic week here-saw excellent craft and artwork, took long walks in the woods, saw plays at various theater festivals, photographic exhibits, etc. Love it! Besides being relaxing and fun, vacations like this sort of rejuvinate the spirit, restore energy, and make one want to try to do something creative.

* * * * *

Someone knocks on your door and says "Help." Chances are that person is pretty unhappy and tried to work out his situation in many ways and might have spoken to several people before he came to you. Most people have to be quite miserable and almost feel driven into therapy. As a therapist, it is important to be as aware as possible of *this individual's* needs, why he came, what he wants and expects from you, your skills (what you feel you

- Gestalt Therapy Verbatim
    Fritz Perls -

- A New Guide for Rational
    Living - Albert Ellis

- The Art of Small Talk -

can do and can't do), whether it's possible to work with this person, whether you feel or don't feel you can do something significant with and for this person. You bring to the session, your intelligence, your sensitivity, your caring, your technical skills (from reading, courses, supervision), your experience (as a result of living and having seen many individuals in therapy). You learn alot, with or without awareness, by just seeing many individuals-with their similarities and differences- and seeing what works and what doesn't work with them. With some people you find that things go better by being patient, understanding and supportive-with others you find you move faster and further by being more direct and assertive, by yelling at them and by showing impatience (rather than understanding) for bullshit and games. Much of this is more difficult to learn intellectually and didacticly than by simply responding to many people and seeing and hearing the outcome of your interactions. I often feel that I've learned a great deal more in the way of helpful therapy by living and experiencing than by reading and taking courses. Although many of these skills come to feel "intuitive", I think that much of this "intuition" is learned, through experience. Skills in communicating and influencing behavior can be put to questionable uses as well as being used to aid people in changing unwanted behaviors and reaching further fulfillment and understanding in their lives. A salesman, for example, could use such interpersonal skills to con someone into buying something he doesn't want or need. A therapist also brings to the therapy situation his sex, race, religion, age, personality, appearance, manner of speech, etc. Such factors also certainly effect how the patient relates to him (how open, closed, comfortable, anxious, structured, informal he will be.)

* * * * *

In addition to personal observation, studies support the notion that patients tend to pick up some of the behavior of their therapists through modeling or imitation. Psychoanalytic patients tend to speak more about their dreams, unconscious motivations, slips of the tongue, fantasies, etc. Rogerian patients (clients) speak increasingly about their feelings and honest reactions to ongoing events. Ellis' rational-emotive patients might curse more (as he does) and speak in terms of "irrational" or "crazy" and "rational" thoughts and behavior. It is unavoidable to bring your self (your personality, behavior, abilities, biases, quirks, moods, theoretical models, etc.) to each session.

* * * * *

Although some things I've recently read by Ram Dass-formerly Richard Alpert-sound really off the wall to me (very possibly my own biases), I agree that it makes good sense to spend alot of time working on yourself, if you want to be a good therapist. I feel the same is true to be a good teacher (at any level.) The more awareness and understanding you have of yourself, your situation, interpersonal relationships, your subject matter, the more likely it is that you will be able to help others to do this with their lives. The main instrument you have in therapy is what you are. (As I write this I'm aware that it has a very "unscientific" ring. Much of my training and work experience have been in the world of science, but I feel that in discussing the "big picture", the whole scene, in an area as complex and encompassing as psychotherapy, this side of the story plays an equally important part.)

* * * * *

Someone says "Help!" I see if we can make a go of it. If I don't think (feel) we can, I suggest that the person might be better off with a woman-black-analyst, etc. You often sense pretty quickly whether or not you can work with someone or if the person might do better with someone else unless you're 1) a dogmatic cultist and feel you can use your theory or model to deal with anybody, 2) so unaware of the patient or yourself that you do not realize that it won't work, 3) very defensive and need to prove to yourself that you can do anything, 4) broke or so eager to make big bucks that the focus is more on keeping the patient than helping him.

* * * * *

As a therapist I feel it's very important to try to put myself in the patient's shoes (to get into his skin) as well as possible in my effort to understand his situation. A distinction can be made between sympathy (feeling the feelings of the patient) and empathy (understanding the person's feelings, but keeping some objective distance, in an effort to be more helpful to him.) If you cry along with the person, you may not be as helpful as you might be if you simply express a sincere understanding and caring about the person's experience, and actively work on alternate behaviors to overcome the sadness. I have found it very valuable to try to recall feelings similar to the patient's when he expresses feelings such as anxiety, confusion, depression, guilt, boredom, etc. John Holt, who wrote a number of beautiful books relating to education, spoke of a situation where he felt very confused and unsure of himself while listening to a famous mathematician who was trying to explain a concept to him. He felt he should be grasping it more quickly and he felt even more uncomfortable when the mathematician was showing impatience over his slowness. Holt said that he recalls those feelings when teaching a child who is not grasping a concept quickly. For the individual who knows the concept well, it might be difficult to understand the other person's confusion. If the teacher feels threatened that he may not be teaching the idea adequately, he might project blame and become even more impatient with the student. By making an effort to recall the experience of such emotions, the therapist can better understand the patient's feelings, and as a result, can more honestly relate to the patient and help him. This is quite similar to what a "method" actor does when playing the part of a person who is experiencing a certain emotion.

Of course, the therapist may not experience the emotion in precisely the same way as the patient. One person may experience "anxiety" primarily in the stomach, while another feels it mainly in the head or in other areas of the body. I think, however, that even making the effort to understand the emotion in this way is beneficial to the therapist, and shows the patient that he is really trying to share or understand his experience.

* * * * *

From time to time patients have expressed concern when they felt it was impossible for me to really understand their particular situation. Some blacks, severely disabled people, and homosexuals have expressed this concern. Some women have also indicated that they felt that as a man I could not truly understand certain feelings of theirs. If the patient's concern over this matter is so great that it interferes with the therapeutic relationship or that it makes him withhold speaking about some topics or feelings, then it could certainly get in the way. If I sense this, then I bring the issue up as a possibility. Generally, however, I feel that if the atmosphere is conducive to being open, if the therapist does not put the person down (overtly or subtly), and if the therapist models honesty and openness of expression, the patient will gradually feel comfortable to discuss such areas quite directly. I also believe that the therapist's honest reply to this concern is important. For example, I might tell a severely handicapped person that while he is right that I have never experienced his disability, I do what I can to project myself into his situation and to understand his feelings as well as possible. As therapy progresses, he will discover for himself whether or not I have some real understanding of his situation and feelings.

* * * * *

As I'm in different situations and places, I often find myself thinking about people I am seeing or have seen in therapy. These thoughts are triggered by aspects of the situation, or by my own ongoing thoughts or feelings at the time. I don't generally push these thoughts-they just happen. Such thoughts often help my identification with or understanding of these people, and sometimes provide ideas for things to work on with them in therapy.

* * * * *

As I'm writing this I find it so difficult not to go on a million tangents-to give more examples, to clarify, or to look at the same situation from many other viewpoints. Therapy is really a terribly complex business. I feel if I indulged in taking many of these tangents, however, it might become boring for both of us, and would probably not really add a great deal to the basic ideas.

* * * * *

Some people become very disturbed by the use of one word over another. While I prefer to refer to someone who comes for therapy as the "person", I will sometimes refer to him as the "patient." This comes from many early learning experiences in the field where these people were generally referred to as "patients." In my case, I probably also use "patient" frequently because of my early experiences working in a medical setting. Some therapists make a big deal out of this because they feel it sounds condescending. I feel that the important factor is your attitude about the person-if you believe that the person who comes for therapy is inferior to the therapist, it doesn't matter whether you call him the "patient", "client", or "person", the underlying attitude will soon become evident during the therapy session. I think it takes alot more than changing a word to make a change in the therapist's attitude.

* * * * *

    I believe that one of the most, if not *the* most, important ingredients of good therapy is honesty. I feel that often direct, blunt honesty is one of the major components that makes psychotherapy different from most other contacts with people, even (perhaps especially) contacts with caring friends and family members. As you're there talking to each other you're both hit with countless possible stimuli, some coming through your senses right then and there (here and now), some thoughts, some feelings, some physical stimuli, etc. As in any other situation, these stimuli can lead to responses, which can be stimuli for further reactions in yourself and in the other person-cognitive or verbal reactions, physical reactions, emotional responses, postural changes, facial expressions. Part of the honesty, is to bring alot of this out into the open, into the awareness of both the patient and therapist.
    You're saying all kinds of nice complimentary stuff to me and smiling, after I just told you that you are intellectualizing about many things that upset you in your life, and that this seems to be something you've been doing for a long time. I then back it up with a bunch of specific events and observations that led me to that statement. Bam! I just hit you with a strong statement which, if you've heard it and processed it are bound to react to in some way. I hear your complimentary words and see your smile, but all kinds of other things can be coming to me at the same time. Maybe your smile was forced and your words sounded mechanical and unreal, maybe I've noticed that whenever I hit you with something direct and challenging you change the subject or try to soften me up, maybe some thought comes to me which competes with my impression about your over-intellectual-

izing and which I feel I'd like to state immediately, maybe I'll respond to the fact that this was one of the first times you've complimented me and I was wondering about your impressions of our sessions, and a million other potential maybe's. I feel that the therapist does best by responding in the manner that seems most direct, meaningful, honest at the time. How you respond is governed by many factors that have been programmed into you as well as by the situation. I believe that if you just say something to be "helpful" or to fill up time or to gain the patient's approval, it will not be as valuable to the person as it would be to express what's hitting you most strongly at the time-even if what's hitting you most strongly is confusion, or boredom, or anger, or feeling manipulated, or feeling helpless at that moment.

You, as therapist (or as an individual) feel more genuine and more comfortable with yourself when you express a thought or a feeling directly, as it is. Of course, the consequences of such a statement may be anger, hostility, defensiveness, withdrawal, etc. on the part of the other person. You are then in a sort of conflict situation in which you are receiving self-reinforcement (and perhaps reinforcement from the other person) for expressing an honest thought or feeling, and punishment (negative feedback from the other person) for the same statement. Perhaps the effect on your behavior will have to do with the balance of the impact of each of these competing consequences on your behavior. And, very probably, your confidence in expressing your next honest reaction (particularly if it's a negative one) will depend also on many other factors at that moment-such as factors in the situation itself, your relationship and feelings regarding the other people present at the time, how ready you feel at the time to put up with negative consequences, your thoughts and feelings about yourself as a result of events immediately preceding the situation, etc.

* * * * *

I don't know if there is something innate or built into people that makes them feel better about themselves when they express themselves honestly or if it has more to do with early learning. Although the "why" is interesting, I suppose the frequent observation that people are generally less comfortable when they express themselves dishonestly than honestly is more important.

* * * * *

Some ideas about how people *learn* to lie:

- When kids tell the truth about something they did or didn't do, differing from their parents' wishes, they might feel they get punished too severely (verbal or physical punishment, or being deprived of some activity they enjoy, etc.) (In this situation, the individual is being *punished* for truthful verbal behavior, and lying results in *escaping* or *avoiding* the aversive reaction of the parents.)

- Kids telling their teachers, or employees telling their bosses about good intentions, or giving excuses for not completing work, often get reinforced for such verbal behavior. (Lying is *reinforced*. Verbal behavior which doesn't coincide with actual behavior often pays off in social situations.)

- People see that when other people lie, the social consequences are often desirable. Kids see this in their parents and in other kids. (In this case, dishonesty is learned through *modeling*-the lying results in reinforcement, and in avoiding punishment. When we look around us we see that verbal behavior often has little relationship with actual behavior.)

- People might discover that when they tell the truth they get much less attention than when they exaggerate and lie. (Telling the truth can gradually be *extinguished*, if we see that lies bring us stronger reinforcements.)

- Kids may start by telling small lies which are reinforced and gradually tell bigger and better lies. (*Shaping*. They can be reinforced for closer and closer approximations to good, big lies.)

* * * * *

People often identify with the heroes in movies and novels, who do what they think, feel, believe, regardless of the social consequences. We get so much advice and encouragement to be ourselves, to do what we truly believe, to be honest, real, genuine, etc. I think most of us can identify with this kind of thinking. It gives us a feeling of freedom. On the other hand, we find that such thinking often leads to aversive consequences. The same parents, teachers, and friends who preach these values ignore us or put us down for saying and doing things against their wishes and demands. Concerning the question of honesty, viewing it as an expression of behavior, we can see how it is encouraged in our culture. It is modeled by heroes and preached by parents, teachers, ministers. It is reinforced in others and ourselves in many arenas, and dishonesty is punished. Because of all of these influences, and perhaps because of other more subtle, innate factors and internal consequences of behaving and expressing ourselves in line with genuine thoughts and feelings, most people come to feel more comfortable, self-satisfied, and relaxed when expressing themselves honestly than dishonestly.

* * * * *

I am pretty much the same person in and out of therapy. My clothes, manner of speech, and basic personality are generally the same in and outside of therapy. I am uncomfortable when I feel I'm acting or playing a role. I have a hard time saying things that I don't really think or feel, or not saying things that I do think or feel. I don't like to and I find myself being uncomfortable and yelling at myself when I act this way. Probably the greatest compromises I make relate to areas like not wearing jeans as much as I would like to in therapy sessions, and cursing a bit less with some patients. If I feel that dressing down or cursing will become too much of an issue and get in the way of *therapy*, I hold back a bit until the person is responding more to *me* and less to the trimmings. I place a very high value on being comfortable and having fun, both in and outside of therapy sessions, and I find this is much more possible when I feel that I'm behaving naturally and spontaneously.

* * * * *

As therapist, you do your best to be in touch

with the person and situation you are in. If you are dealing with a very disturbed, anxious, depressed person, you often won't be having too much fun in there. With such a person I usually feel concerned, empathetic, eager to do something to help the situation, but even with such individuals I find that being relaxed and maintaining a sense of humor are generally appreciated. If I'm working with a conservative, elderly person, I won't generally go out of my way to dress down or say words like "shit" too much because it might well get in the way of our relating to each other. On the other hand, I won't hold back on expressing basic thoughts, or feelings, or impressions that I have along the way.

* * * * *

Acceptance of yourself and of the other person are very important aspects of therapy. Feeling happy, depressed, relaxed, anxious, guilty, bored, confident, confused, angry, etc. are all very real, natural feelings, and everyone feels these emotions, the good ones and the bad ones. This includes all people labled *normal and healthy* as well as those labled *emotionally disturbed*. Although people often easily accept the "good" feelings, unless they are punishing themselves for something, many escape, avoid, or deny the uncomfortable ones. One of the useful things that can be done in therapy is to help a person to accept that the crummy feelings are okay too, unless those are the only ones. Often being aware of and accepting all of one's feelings is one of the first steps in feeling better about one's self. Accepting one's own negative feelings also helps one to understand and accept such feelings in other people.

* * * * *

Many individuals seem to be out of touch with- or alienate-the animal and child in themselves when acceptance of these parts of their total selves can add so much to the understanding and enjoyment of their lives.

* * * * *

So many people I have seen in therapy feel that they are different from others and don't fit into the world. Anything I can say or do to show them how I or others can understand and honestly feel some of the same uncomfortable feelings is usually helpful. I believe that while we are all different in many ways (e.g. abilities, interests, attitudes, values, personality, appearance, etc.), we are essentially very much the same underneath (e.g. our basic feelings, the ways we learn, our real needs, etc.)

* * * * *

This morning I saw Don, a sixteen year old kid for the second time. His father deserted the family when he was an infant, and his mother is a very disturbed woman who has been in and out of mental hospitals for years. He was a foster child for the past two years. Although he is bright, he is very shy and reserved, particularly with strangers. He came to therapy because he was "sent", and he made it clear from the start that he didn't want to be there. After talking to his foster mother for fifteen or twenty minutes, I saw him and started talking about his problems-e.g. How does he feel about his mother? Why did he put tattoos on his body with a pin and India ink saying such things as "Fuck You" on his forearm and "Kill" across his fingers?, etc. He made it very clear that this was none of my business, and that the only reason he came was because he had to. He asked "What's it to you?" and "Why are you snooping like this?" Someone like Don is called "resistant" in the trade. He doesn't want to be there and he presents himself as if to say "Here I am-You're the doctor-Do something." This is really quite common among people who are sent to therapy, and have reservations about being there. For example: 1) children who don't feel anything is wrong with them and their parents send them, 2) husbands or wives whose spouses say that if they don't go to therapy, they will leave, 3) homosexuals, alcoholics, etc., who are basically comfortable with their lives, but are pressured to enter therapy, 4) people in hospitals or who are ordered by courts or other agencies to undergo psychotherapy when they do not feel the need for it, etc. My feeling is that people generally accept and do best in therapy when they initiate it or are driven into it by very uncomfortable feelings or a strong desire to do something about themselves and their lives.

After seeing that during our first session I obviously bombed out by immediately confronting Don with topics that were very uncomfortable for him to talk about, 1) I told him how I thought therapy might be of some value to him-i.e. that he would have the chance to talk to someone about things that bothered him, but that he didn't like to talk to other people about, and that our sessions would be strictly confidential and 2) I told him to think about it a little more and wait a week or two before making a final decision on the matter. Then, I set up another appointment.

During our second session, after the first few minutes, which were quite unproductive, I asked Don if he wanted to play a game of chess and he said okay. Toward the end of the previous session, when I saw we were getting nowhere fast, I suggested that we might play chess and he quickly said that he'd make a deal with me-if he beat me in chess, he wouldn't have to return for another session. Hearing that kind of confidence, and being fully aware of my modest skills in the game, I wisely refused his offer. When we played chess this morning, he destroyed me. He didn't just take my key men, but aggressively knocked the pieces off the board as he took them. I spent most of the session laying back, openly admiring good moves, and did little therapizing. He appeared to enjoy the session, and we left on much better terms than we did after our first encounter. I think he may be a little more open next session, but I will still tread easy with him until I see that he is more willing to open up about more sensitive matters.

I don't like to twist someones arm into therapy. Since I often hit it off reasonably well with people in therapy, I can tolerate it if now and then someone is not too enthusiastic about the situation or me. I have found that if a patient is resistant to therapy, it's often worth spending a few sessions trying to get a relationship going, telling him very honestly what value it may be, and briefly discussing what therapy is and isn't about. If you win the person over and get him involved, great-if not, and therapy seems advisable, then you just let him know that the door is open if he should choose to return. To spend alot of time trying to motivate the person for therapy is generally futile, but I have found that it is often useful to ease up, try to make contact, and give a direct, honest appraisal of the situation to the individual before letting go.

* * * * *

    I just got back from a fantastic photographic exhibit at the Museum of Modern Art in Manhattan. It was a large collection of the works of Harry Callihan. Photography has long been an interest of mine. I started going places to take pictures and doing my own developing and printing when I was about thirteen or fourteen. In recent years I especially enjoy going to exhibits at the International Center for Photography and at the Museum of Modern Art. Although I do not regard photography as a primary art in the sense of painting or sculpting where one is taking a blank canvas or clump of clay and making something out of nothing with his own imagination and technical skills, I enjoy looking at photographs as an artistic expression as much as anything. It is an interest which I enjoy both doing and observing.
    Callihan has a great eye for composition in nature as well as for capturing human moments. His nature pictures have an abstract quality-fascinating forms and use of space. He makes it very interesting and exciting to look at the world through his eyes. I found it particularly enjoyable because in my photographic work, I am primarily interested in capturing moments in people and in natural abstracts. In addition to his interesting range of subject matter, his technique and craftsmanship were excellent.
    I feel that anything that adds to one's enjoyment in daily living has considerable value and adds meaning to one's life. When I talk to some very depressed patients and people who seem to find everything to me meaningless, I often feel genuine concern, but try to search for sparks of potential areas of interest and involvement. An existentialist's view of living stresses the anxiety one experiences over a sense of meaningless-

ness, and expresses the fact that nothing has a built-in absolute meaning or value. They say that one has to determine his own meanings in life-"existence before essence." I believe that many of an individual's meanings are learned through experiences. The more one experiments and is exposed to things and to people who are excited about things, the more opportunities one finds for new sources of interest and meaning. For me photography and photographs have meaning, probably due to many factors in my behavioral history (e.g. seeing parents' interest, being exposed to art and music alot during my childhood, dabbling in photography and enjoying it.) To someone else, this particular area of interest might have little meaning, and very different areas might have great meaning to him while they have no real, personal meaning for me. Whether one acquires a new area of interest and source of meaning by choice or by learning experiences (an important question for many), the point is that by aiding a patient in exploring new sources of interest and involvement that might click for him, you help that person to add a sense of meaning to his life. Often we stumble into new sources of meaningfulness quite by accident.

I see several ways in which photography is analagous to working in psychotherapy. In good psychotherapy, as in good photography, one of the main activities is to look at the same subject matter or situation from many different angles or viewpoints. The patient like the viewer can experience a sense of "Hey, I never looked at it or thought about it in that way before." Psychotherapists, like photographers, have a wide range of individual styles, points of emphasis, stresses on technique or minimizing the importance of technique. In both, sometimes the "other" can feel a tremendous identification with the "doer" or can feel little rapport. In both, the "other" might gain by looking at things through the eyes of the "doer." Some therapists and photographers are more versatile than others, some experiment a great deal with new approaches, while others stay basically with one approach and subject matter. Both can be very creative and alive.

* * * * *

    Looking at a situation from different angles and viewpoints can be of great value to many patients, particularly if you sense that they are quite rigid in their approach to problems. This approach is probably not as useful to those who tend to be confused and think continuously of alternative possibilities in a situation, and don't think seriously enough about any of them to place more weight on more realistic or desirable ones. Such "spoilers" need more in the way of really sticking with a problem and thinking it through, rather than setting up one possibility after another and knocking it down. But, more frequently, people seem to get locked into a sort of tunnel vision and don't view a problem in other ways.
    Another way of expressing this is to view therapy, in some cases, as helping to re-conceptualize the patient's view of his problem. Sometimes this can make even one or two sessions with a patient very effective, if he really comes to see his situation in a more workable way.

* * * * *

    Although the problems of searching for meaning and finding everything to be meaningless have certainly been struggled with by people throughout history, these areas continue to be major causes for people to seek therapy. Perhaps in an age of looser roots, relationships and family ties, specialization, many mundane jobs which people cannot take pride in and identify with, many passive pastimes (e.g. watching sports, T.V.), increased crime, etc., people find it even harder to find meaning in their lives than in previous generations. Although we all wrestle with such problems at times in our lives, many people seek therapy when the feelings of anxiety, despair, and depression accompanying their sense of meaninglessness feel overwhelming.

The following are some typical conditions under which I have seen people in therapy due to their sense of meaninglessness: Teenagers and people in their early twenties who have had early learned values seriously challenged or shattered (e.g. religious values, sexual values, etc.). Young people who have found that they will not be able to attain idealized goals (e.g. can't obtain grades to be admitted into desired programs, insufficient money to enter desired programs, minority members discriminated against, etc.). Loss of a loved one (e.g. death, person leaves, etc.). People who have attained a goal after working hard to reach it-educationally, vocationally, monetarily, status-wise and then feel that something important is still missing. Loss of work that one identified closely with. People who upon thinking about the finality of death consequently see life's activities as meaningless.

To attempt to systematically desensitize (a conditioning procedure) this kind of anxiety is generally not of any real value to the person. Trying to convince the person that things are meaningful is also futile as a rule. Again, therapy has to focus on the individual's particular dilemma. When the sense of meaninglessness is reactive to a real event in the person's life, helping him to accept that part of the issue is living through the feelings, and allowing some time to go by, is often valuable. Searching for sparks of interest and meaning to build on is also useful with many people. Once an individual finds one real source of meaning (such as a close relationship with someone, or an activity which excites the person's interest and involvement), the sense of meaningfulness often carries over to other areas. Experimenting with new potential areas of interest is often valuable.

In working with patients who speak of suicide because of their sense of meaninglessness, therapy generally includes working with the person to understand that the despairing feelings are rarely permanent, along with exploring potential areas of meaning in the person's life. In dealing with this problem, I feel it is also very important for the therapist to convey a real understanding of the person's desperate thoughts and feelings, and to make it evident to the patient that he, himself, has areas of real meaning in his own life. The relationship formed with such a patient is particularly important.

* * * * *

I try not to kill a person's passion for living during therapy. A big part of the job is often to increase excitement and interest in things. I've seen some people who have undergone long-term deeply analytic therapies lose a great deal of their excitement and crazy (in the good sense) qualities. I often like wild, nutty people, who feel passionately about things and ideas. By making therapy too analytical and explanitory, and highly intellectualized, there is a real danger of taking some of the life out of a person.

The psychiatrist in the play "Equus" felt over-intellectualized and was jealous of the passionate feelings of the young man he was treating. He said he would have given anything to feel the way that boy felt just for a short time. I personally know therapists who are over-intellectualized, lifeless, and feel boxed-in, but I don't feel this is necessary. It very probably stands in the way of therapy. I believe that it adds to therapy if the therapist is genuinely lively, enthusiastic, and gets excited over things. I don't like the idea of being pushed into the role of solid, stable, conservative, benevolent, machine-like, wise old healer. I prefer *human* beings, and I think that a *human* model in the therapy situation is much more beneficial to the patient.

* * * * *

I generally feel happier and better about myself when I am behaving spontaneously and naturally, rather than thinking and planning too much. This goes for my behavior while working, as well as when spending time on hobbies and interests, or talking to people in formal or informal settings. Of course, it is much harder to be spontaneous in some situations than others. Whenever we're with other people, even with just one other person, things that we say might be disagreed with, ignored, laughed at, etc. Even if we are quite confident about a thought, unless we are defensive or insensitive to the thoughts and feelings of those around us, we are often affected by these reactions. This happens despite the encouragement in essays, novels, movies, etc. to identify with the character who looks within himself for his answers, and is not strongly affected by the negative reactions of others. I have found that if someone gets a good amount of reinforcement for his skills, thoughts, behavior in at least one area, it will often help that person to behave more independently and spontaneously, at least in some other areas as well.

* * * * *

When my behavior is spontaneous while giving a lecture in a classroom or while in a therapy session, I generally feel better about my behavior during the situation and after it is completed, although there is always an element of risk in this spontaneity. There is a certain comfort in having a good set of organized notes to refer to in a classroom situation, or of having a prepared "plan of attack" in a therapy session. I have found, however, that I generally feel best when I am more tuned in to the situation, to my spontaneous thoughts and feelings at the time, and to the ongoing reactions of the other person (or people.) The risk is that at times you leave a situation feeling that you would have done a more effective job if you were more structured and put more time into organization. Particularly, if you're teaching a class about subject matter that you don't know thoroughly, or are working with a patient who needs considerable structure in dealing with his problem, a more spontaneous approach may cause considerable discomfort. Nevertheless, I have found that expressing thoughts, feelings, and ongoing reactions, more often than not results in a good, alive feeling. No matter how you teach or conduct therapy sessions, sometimes you're going to leave the situation feeling you just didn't make it or that you weren't on the same wavelength as the people you're relating to. Fortunately, having some good experiences being spontaneous in these situations helps to overcome the temporary discomfort following those that don't work out so well. Such an approach helps to keep you more involved and interested than a safer, highly structured approach. Most of us have had teachers who have said and done pretty nearly the same things for years in teaching a given course-the same examples, the same jokes-this follows this-follows this-deadly-boring, you can see it in their presentation-and feel it. The person is out of touch with himself and you at the time.

* * * * *

Although I find myself thinking about one patient or another at almost any time, before I see someone in therapy, I generally loosely prepare for each session. That is, I briefly review previous sessions and jot down some thoughts about topics we might continue to work on, or new areas we might explore. But, even with such preparation, I try to enter the session with flexibility, and let the apparent needs of the person dictate what we do. I think it's important to leave room for constructive-not avoiding or defensive-tangents which might lead to important places.

* * * * *

I love experiences that free the spirit-that make me feel alive, free, unrestricted, and I often try to bring this feeling to my therapy sessions. I like crazy, off beat comedians, who show people that it's okay to break out of rigid, conforming social roles and behaviors, and experiment with other behaviors. I get some of the same feelings when listening to some music, seeing some paintings and sculpture, reading some books, watching some movies and plays, traveling to different places and experiencing different cultures. I also get a certain liberating feeling while working on some of my interests-photography, sketching, playing the piano and guitar, playing tennis.

* * * * *

As long as I can remember I've loved new experiences. I've always found them to be revitalizing and enriching in learning more about people and life. The following is a brief entry from a log I kept when I worked on a Norwegian freighter, during the summer when I was nineteen. The ship went down the Orinoco and Amazon Rivers to transport iron ore.

July 19, 1957

This morning after being awoken at 5:45 by the human alarm clock, I went on deck to see an incredible sunrise. The sun, just rising over the horizon, made the clouds glisten like diamonds. I can think of no better atmosphere for thinking about life and nature than the sea. Looking out on the water and sky makes one feel so significant, in a way, knowing that he is alive while all this isn't; on the other hand, it makes one feel extremely insignificant, realizing that what is *he* next to all this.

Yesterday morning, the steward called me out onto the deck while I was in the middle of serving breakfast. Several hundred pound dolphins were following the ship. I was amazed to see these huge creatures leaping several feet out of the water. He told me that since dolphins are among the fastest salt water animals, they would have little trouble following the boat for quite a distance.

I just finished reading the translations of *170 Chinese Poems*. I was impressed by their tremendous appreciation for life and nature. Chinese poetry apparently differs from American poetry mainly in that the poet is not so much a lover as a friend. He tends to regard himself as a simple friend, with no great ambition, plenty of free time, and an appreciation for simple living.

I've just started to read *Two Years Before the Mast,* a true journal of the voyage of Dana, at age twenty, who wanted to place himself in an entirely different environment for awhile.

I can understand why about five of the world's top ten classics are sea stories. There is something about the atmosphere that is like a fairy tale, and yet it is real.

My roommate is a twenty four year old guy from Philadelphia. Up to this point, he has been a high school teacher, a cadet at West Point for a year, and recently, a translator for the government. He says that his friends all told him he was crazy for giving up his last job, which paid so well, to take a job at sea. But, right now he is not looking for security; he wants to enjoy himself. He says that because of his education he can always make money. He reads alot (mostly in Spanish), writes plays (of which, as yet, I have read none), and plays the guitar well (classical and flamenco.) He's been teaching me some new chord progressions and strums.

The sea looks much different than it did for the last week or so; it is much flatter, and the ripples are going in all different directions. This I was told indicates that the current is great. This is due to the breaking up and rejoining of currents by the islands. So far I've only seen one fishing boat. The steward said it was because the people are lazy.

* * * * *

In working with patients, I feel that I generally relate to the person primarily as a *person* and not as a male, female, black, white, child, adult, American, European, Christian, Jew, rich, poor, etc. I like Harry Stack Sullivan's thought that basically we are all more human than otherwise. Of course, these are words, and while saying such things I can really be more bigoted or chauvinistic than I am aware of while actually in a therapy situation. As much as possible, I try to see the people as they are, try to give them feedback on these perceptions, try to encourage them to grow in directions they wish to grow, and become what they can become. I have a great respect for the uniqueness of each individual, and I really dislike putting people into stereotypes. Although I may personally enjoy, admire, or be attracted to some patients much more than others, I try not to let these natural (and learned) personal reactions interfere with the business at hand. If I feel that such personal reactions are interfering with therapy, I bring it out into the open, and if I see that we can't deal with and overcome the issue, I refer the person to someone else.

* * * * *

    While I understand the preoccupation of some people with their femaleness, blackness, etc. and their concern about being abused and maltreated, I've seen many people hide behind such issues and use them to rationalize their personal failures and problems and prevent themselves from taking responsibility to improve their lives. I don't mean to minimize the serious oppression, indignities, and conditioned self-hatred that have been experienced by such groups through the years. But, to hang onto the anger and alienate oneself from the world on the basis of identifying with a particular group, appears to me to be self-defeating and a waste of time. I often question the real motivation of people who devote a tremendous portion of their energies to yelling at the world for screwing up their lives.

* * * * *

    I am very attracted to a "here-now" approach to living. Reading and thinking about it and practicing it as well as I could has been a valuable experience. Discussing a here-now life style with patients and working with many of them to live more in this manner has frequently been helpful. The suggestion of Frederick Perls (founder of Gestalt Therapy) to "lose your mind and come to your senses" has been influential.
    Many people greatly increase their anxiety, depression, or sense of meaninglessness by living more in the past or future, or in their minds, than in the present. They dwell on past bad experiences, and what they should have done, or spend a great deal of time planning what they should do,

or will do, or hope to do in the future. When alot of energy is put into such activities, little is left over for living here and now-for really being here with all of your senses. You can't be fully experiencing and enjoying what you're doing, if you're not all there at that time.

Some of the good points of a "here-now" approach are that it allows you to experience ongoing situations more completely, it gives you more available energy to put into present situations, it takes your thinking away from fearful thoughts which could interfere with your enjoyment of a situation. Many people get very hung up on their thoughts and get so lost in the process of thinking that they cannot really be open to behaving naturally. These covert words (that people are saying to themselves) intensify anxiety, depression, self-consciousness, lack of confidence, feelings of meaninglessness, etc. People often find it helpful to get involved in many activities when they feel depressed, partly because keeping busy and involved competes with thoughts that are keeping them down.

On the other side of this, however, are some questionable aspects of here-now living. I have seen it used as a defense, to escape from or avoid really thinking a problem through. Sometimes, staying with one's feelings of meaninglessness, or thinking through a situation that one was not pleased with in the past, or sticking with difficult thoughts about what to do in a future situation is very important. Although leaving these thoughts for the here-now might offer relief from such uncomfortable thinking, it could also prevent the person from working through some important areas in his life. While helping one to the *awareness* of what he is doing here and now (in terms of motor behavior, thinking, verbal behavior, posture, voice quality, etc.) can be very valuable to a person in understanding himself better, encouraging one to *live* only in the here and now could be encouraging a defense.

* * * * *

Although living mostly in one's fantasy world is generally considered *crazy* behavior, leaving the here and now to enter one's fantasy world for a short time when one is bored, depressed or anxious can be rejuvinating. It helps to return to the present with more energy and confidence. Although an *awareness* of what you are doing here and now includes being aware of when and how you are avoiding or escaping uncomfortable feelings, to overdo pushing yourself into here and now *ongoing activities* can be a defense competing with the awareness of such things.

* * * * *

So much of what I read in the psychology literature seems boring and uncreative to me. So much is repetitive, obvious, dry as dust, or just shows one more slight variation of a procedure. Looking at the many journals and convention programs is often very uninspiring.

Of course, there's nothing wrong with devoting years to one small area of study, and carefully examining the effects on behavior of slight changes in stimuli and procedures. Such activities help to build a science. There are many well known, highly respected psychologists who have done this, as well as equally known people who have varied their areas of study greatly over time. There's lots of room for people to follow their own paths. At this point in my life, I prefer to read, think about, search for, and act on new things. I like to draw from different areas and think about events from different angles and perspectives. I personally find this a more exciting way to approach both research and therapy sessions, as well as teaching classes and living in general. I like Picasso's thought: "If you know exactly what you are going to do, what's the good of doing it? There's no interest in something you know already. It's much better to do something else." While it is safe to stay on firm ground and to keep your thinking confined to comfortable and known ways, this can be deadly to one's spirit.

Psychology-the study (or science) of behavior-is an immensely broad field and even at this early stage, it is impossible to know more than a small fraction of the literature. So, a student of the field has to make some careful choices as to what to focus on, and read, and think about, unless he wishes to just taste many areas and not really know any well.

* * * * *

When I saw Marlon Brando on a television interview, he spoke about the problems of Indians in this country and all kinds of things that interested and concerned him, but he did everything under the sun to avoid talking about acting. When he finally spoke about it briefly, he said that it was a craft and that he didn't like to talk about it much. It's true that to get down to the nitty-gritty of almost anything is much more complex than it appears to be on the surface, and to touch the surface of something often just doesn't do justice to the subject. I have found this to be very true of psychotherapy. Tennessee Williams, in his autobiography, also said that he doesn't like to discuss his craft very much; he just loves to do it. Henry Moore expressed a similar thought regarding his work. Ernest Hemingway said that he didn't spend too much time with other writers because he often found it boring to discuss work. Although I have some close psychologist friends, most of my friends are not psychologists. Discussing involved things that concern you deeply in a superficial or limited way can really be a drag. I've sure found this to be true in the behavior business. With most people there are lots of things I'd rather discuss than the hairy, theoretical end of psychology.

* * * * *

    I find it very valuable in therapy to put myself in the place of people I am working with, to try to really understand how they are feeling in their situations. Although this is sometimes emotionally exhausting, it helps in several ways. First, the patient senses that you are trying to understand him in a real way, not just in some hard-assed, cold, objective, analytical way. Second, it gives alternate ideas of how you might deal with the situation-ideas from procedures and methods you have studied, ideas that seemed effective with other patients in similar situations, and intuitive ideas.
    By putting yourself in the shoes of *other* significant people in the patient's world, as you learn more about these people, it allows you to gain and convey a better understanding of them to the patient. It also shows that the process of seriously putting one's self in the place of another can increase understanding, and often acceptance, of that person. The Gestalt therapy procedure of having the patient play the two roles of

the other person and himself in an ongoing situation-conversing back and forth-and then, asking the patient what he is feeling and thinking at key times, is very valuable in fostering understanding of oneself and others.

* * * * *

One of the most useful approaches for understanding and communicating with patients is to discuss matters with an attitude of "I *feel* and *think* ----, and You *feel* and *think* ----" in an open, accepting atmosphere. Rogers discussed this approach extremely well in his book *On Becoming a Person*. This underlying attitude is helpful whether it is overtly expressed or not. It continuously directs your attention to both your own thoughts and feelings and those of the other person, and helps to bring into the open and to contrast any differences during the session. It is particularly valuable in establishing honest and open communication, if it is done with a spirit of understanding and accepting both sides, even if the other person's reactions differ greatly from your own. If you are wrong when expressing to the patient what you sense his thoughts or feelings are, he will generally correct you and give you a more accurate picture of what is going on in him.

Without genuine sensitivity to a patient's thoughts and feelings, the distance between therapist and patient increases. The patient increasingly feels a lack of understanding and caring on the part of the therapist. For some people, seeing that someone is listening and *hearing* is one of the most important aspects of therapy.

* * * * *

A therapist must use judgment as to when to disclose personal thoughts and feelings, and he certainly shouldn't overdo it. The primary focus belongs on the patient. I have found, however, that disclosing some personal reactions or events in my life has been particularly useful in opening up some people who were initially very reluctant to let me into their private worlds.

* * * * *

As Abraham Maslow pointed out, one difficulty in approaching patients with too much of a Taoistic "let be", non-judgmental attitude, is that this could lead to the danger of inaction or indecision. Although it is extremely valuable to be understanding and accepting of the person, carrying this to an extreme could, at times, stand in the way of change. Larry, in O'Neill's *The Iceman Cometh*, explained that his main problem was that of being too understanding of all sides. There have been times when I could really identify with this.

* * * * *

Freida Fromm-Reichmann's suggestion, in *Principles of Intensive Psychotherapy*, to be expecially gentle with certain "schizophrenics" was helpful in working with Marie. If I came on too strong with her initially, it would have scared the hell out of her. Although I've learned some helpful things about treating individuals with particular *psychodiagnostic labels* from some sources, generally, I've found it much more valuable to 1) tune in to the individual person as well as I could, and 2) draw from sources that provided ideas for understanding and doing something about changing specific behaviors or emotional responses. A wide range of people fit under most psychodiagnostic labels. While classification may be helpful to give a general idea of the nature and severity of a person's disturbance, to appropriately place people in certain situations, to get financial support from insurance companies, government agencies, or other sources, or to give some general ideas about treatment; most often, I do not find that the psychodiagnostic classification helps me to understand or work with a person much more effectively. Another problem with labeling children or adults in this way is that the labels often tend to follow the person and influence future people that the individual comes in contact with (or negatively effect the individual, himself.)

* * * * *

Having a psychotherapy practice in the suburbs comes with some assets and liabilities. Some of the good points are that there are plenty of people to draw from, many people are "psychology-minded" and are not overly resistant to going to a therapist. On the other hand, since the cost of living is higher than in more rural areas, the psychologist may feel pressured to see more people and take on more outside responsibilities than he wishes, in order to meet his expenses.

I really like a slice of life practice-males and females of varied ages, backgrounds, races, religions, occupations and socio-economic levels. In a suburban practice, if you wish to see a cross section of people and not limit your practice to the more affluent, it is necessary to take steps to obtain referrals from state agencies or make it known that you have a sliding scale of fees to accomodate people who cannot afford the usual rates. Fortunately, insurance companies are also increasingly covering a significant portion of psychologists' fees.

Living and working in an area like Wayne, New Jersey has given me the opportunity to be immersed in and observe suburban living. I see a great deal of plastic and superficial living; the lack of depth in personal values and philosophies; the pressures on people to make "big bucks" to meet the high cost of living; the frustration of many housewives trying to enjoy their families and their own lives while feeling the boredom and frustration of many necessary but unchallenging chores; the high value placed on material possessions and the frustration of people who constantly feel they want more; the turn to alcohol and extra-marital affairs to escape from the pressures of daily life; and the high divorce rate to escape from unsatisfying marriages or in search of something better. I also see the effects on the children in these families.

Some of the benefits of living in such an area are that my children have loads of kids to be with, there are a wide variety of activities to get involved in, we are near Manhattan which offers all kinds of entertainment and cultural things to do, and we have found our children's schools and teachers to be quite good for the most part. I regret that our children do not have more experiences with people of more diverse backgrounds. Although Diane and I talk about kids of other backgrounds and try to encourage openness and understanding, I feel that perhaps growing up and personally experiencing a broader range of people might be necessary for a real understanding and ability to form relationships with a wide variety of people.

As a psychologist in the suburbs, my referrals come from a variety of sources-from undergraduate and graduate students I have taught, from state agencies (The New Jersey Division of Youth and Family Services and the Division of Vocational Rehabilitation), from schools and from physicians. I like the fact that my best source of new patients has been other patients. Without referral resources, a therapist can get pretty lonesome. As I'm in practice longer, I find people coming from many different directions, and I'm generally busier than I care to be.

One source of aggravation along these lines is the relative sparseness of referrals to psychologists from physicians. Physicians in many specialties are in a position to do a great deal of very indicated referring to psychologists. Although some do, many state openly that they automatically refer to psychiatrists. One pediatrician in town told me that he always referred to psychiatrists because he was sort of "brainwashed in medical school to believe that only people in the medical profession really knew what they were doing." I know others who do some referring only to personal friends. I've seen situations where psychologists got referrals from physicians after years of association with a psychiatrist (that is, where they shared a practice, and initially did the psychiatrist's testing or saw some of his overload patients.) I've also seen some psychologists who have apparently received referrals from physicians on the basis of their attractive offices, stylish wardrobes, and market-place personality styles. This kind of bullshit particularly gets to me.

* * * * *

Being a local bigshot was never one of my aspirations. So many "professional" people in the suburbs seem to be into this kind of thinking. I like my work and when I see that things are going well I feel good. Playing bigshot seems phoney to me and takes alot of energy that might be put to better use.

* * * * *

There are always a great variety of problems in people of different ages, due to different behavioral histories and situations. In my practice, I have seen a common pattern of typical, general problems in people of different ages which brings them to therapy, however.

Often children are brought to therapy by their parents because of behavior problems at school and in the home. They act out, are not cooperative, are hyperactive, too shy, too aggressive, or don't get along with other children. In recent years, many children also enter therapy because of problems resulting from the breaking up of families.

Adolescents, generally part child-part adult, are often seeking independence, have difficulty in communicating with their parents, and are searching for meaning, direction, and identity. They are often especially concerned about relating to peers and particularly male-female relationships.

People in their twenties are frequently concerned about love relationships, sexual difficulties, searching for meaning and identity, or establishing vocational goals and security.

I have seen many people in their thirties who have more or less reached their basic educational, vocational and family goals and are essentially where they were aiming and working to be in life, but feel something is missing—"there must be more." They are often concerned about sexual problems, marital problems, their children, considerations about seeking different employment, difficulties in relationships, or finding new areas of interest.

Often problems of people in their forties center around accepting themselves as they are, after seeing that it is unlikely that they will achieve some of their dreams for wealth, status, etc. It is frequently a problem of acceptance of one's general life situation or planning a change. Many also have difficulty with letting go of youth and accepting their age.

Many people in their fifties and over are concerned with decreasing abilities, losing work, losing loved friends and relatives, or dealing with the reality of increasing ill health and death. There is often a need to find real interests to substitute for past work and relationships. Dealing with depression is a common problem presented by people in this age range.

Of course, these are impressions. This is not a carefully studied, research-based, comprehensive list of life crises, and there are many individual differences. But, while everyone presents individual problems, the degree of similarity in problems experienced at various age levels is remarkable.

* * * * *

Tom was greatly helped by the Triavil (a combination antidepressant and tranquilizer) he began taking about six weeks ago. Without this drug he might have quit his job, as an executive in a large advertising agency, and probably would have been much more difficult to work with in therapy. It got the edge off his depression and anxiety, helped him to cope, and aided him in settling down to think his problems through and deal with them in therapy. I don't believe that drugs, by themselves, generally make lasting, important changes, and don't see them as a substitute for facing and taking responsibility for dealing with personal problems. They might help, however, to get a person in a state where he can, for a time, function better and work on the difficulties. As a psychologist, I cannot prescribe drugs, but I have generally found the person's physician to be cooperative in prescribing drugs when they seemed indicated. I don't generally consider recommending drugs unless the person appears to be in a pretty bad way, and I feel strongly that medication might be helpful to keep the person functioning through a crisis situation, or to work on his problems better. It is a course of action that I am slow to suggest. I prefer to see the person try to work on things without drugs first when possible. Although some psychiatrists believe that drugs will eventually be "the answer" to most problems encountered by people in therapy, I will have to see some very solid research reports and evidence to be convinced. I have seen too many people whose problems clearly relate to their life experiences, and who have been greatly helped by understanding and dealing directly with their problems.

Although I am very slow to recommend incorporating medication into the therapy plan, I have seen cases where it was very helpful. At times, people are quick to put down the possible benefits of such drugs before giving them a chance. I have encountered parents of neurologically impaired children who have done this with Ritalin, for example. Too small a dosage resulted in no noticable changes. Too large a dose made some children sleepy or zombie-like. Often the effective dosage has to be discovered through trial and error, and then has to be monitored over time, to make sure that the drug is being tailored effectively to the child. I have seen cases where drugs like Ritalin have been very helpful, just as I have found tranquilizers and antidepressants to be useful adjuncts to therapy with some people. You don't want to throw out the baby with the bath water. I have found it best to try to gear the entire therapy to the needs of the individual.

* * * * *

Although I learn and get inspired by reading and find reading a great escape from daily routine, during periods of reading less I often find myself more open to ongoing experiences and doing my own thinking. So much of the business of doing therapy comes from what you learn by doing and experiencing. The more experiences you have and work through, the better position you are in to understand the lives and problems of your patients. If you lead a sheltered, safe, uneventful existence, it is less likely that you will be able to identify with and really understand many of the people and problems confronting you in therapy.

* * * * *

You learn a great deal about living from your patients. You see all kinds of emotions at their extremes, see all sorts of life styles, and learn about limitless experiences and personal philosophies. Everyone has his own unique story, and his own ways of looking at things. If you're open, you learn alot. One of the great things about a good therapy relationship is the high degree of honest communication, hopefully both ways. There are so many factors which make honest communication very difficult in most situations. People are trying to impress, or play a certain role, or don't want to expose weaknesses, or don't want to express experiences which will lead to hassles or punishment, or reveal embarrasing thoughts or feelings. In therapy, one of my ground rules is to try to cut through the bullshit and try to get to what's really happening, as well as possible. In this context, both the patient and therapist can learn a great deal about themselves.

* * * * *

It seems entirely possible to me that some of the best therapists may be unknown people who have never been inclined to write, and that some prolific and popular writers in this field may themselves be mediocre therapists. The abilities to theorize, explain, and do, don't necessarily go together.

* * * * *

Who are you? Are you a psychotherapist comparing your thoughts, feelings, and perceptions with mine? Are you a student trying to get some idea of what a practicing psychologist does and thinks about in relation to his work? Are you a person seeking self-help or curious about what at least one psychotherapist does and thinks about? I know I'm writing this book alot for me, but I'm also writing it very much for you. I'm writing quite personally and honestly.
    I can see why some people reading these notes might find certain parts a real drag-perhaps, parts like this. I'm writing from different places in me and about a pretty wide variety of things-I'm talking about the work of a therapist, specifics about the art, craft, science, and philosophy of

therapy, the patient and the therapist, and I'm talking about me-my reactions and experiences and how they might relate to my work. Some people may be quite interested in some aspects and have very little interest in others-it depends alot on where you are coming from. We all have our own particular interests. I have always enjoyed the dimension of knowing something about the person behind the words and thoughts I am reading.

* * * * *

Creativity is a fascinating subject. Although it is difficult to define, I have generally thought of creativity in two basic ways. One view concerns the notion of coming up with something new and original-which is a very difficult thing to do. So much of what we do or think about has been done or thought about before. Another view concerns looking at the same phenomenon from different angles or viewpoints. In the arts this is often clear. People can look at the same subject matter very differently. Coming up with something really new and different is a rarity. While we all fantasize about new and different things, we seldom put enough energy into these things to make them real. Concerning the second view of creativity, it is often fascinating to view things and events from different angles. Thinking about creativity in this way relates to many different vocations as well as to creativity in daily living. The capacity to look at a given situation in different ways often adds a great deal to one's understanding of and potency in that situation.

In the arts one sees how such a view is relevant. It is exciting for the artist and the viewer to experience fresh points of view. Artists, authors, composers, photographers, playwrights, singers, dancers, and comedians can help us to see that situations can be viewed in many ways. But, we can be creative in many other areas of life. When a scientific researcher considers a given phenomenon in different ways, he might come up with a finding that can interest or benefit us all. In psychotherapy, if the therapist is capable of looking at a problem from different angles, it may show the patient that he is not locked into a given viewpoint. Rigidity and consistency might lead to a degree of predictability and security, but it may trap a person from seeing alternatives. In most situations, there are other ways of looking at and doing what we're doing. Creativity is very relevant to many kinds of work, to interpersonal relationships, and to living in general.

* * * * *

I really enjoy reading things by and about such artists as Paul Klee, Vasili Kandinski, and Henry Moore because of their integrity, creativity, and the depth of their thinking about their work. Although these individuals were unusually aware of their surroundings and experiences, they generally searched deep within themselves for the source of their creativity and originality, and found this internal focus to be more powerful and meaningful than sources outside themselves.
Although I like to struggle with stuff like this, I don't impose such thinking on my patients during sessions unless it seems relevant. During therapy, their stuff (needs and concerns) is more important to focus on.

* * * * *

Many *pop psychology* books tell us that we can do anything we want if we want to do it badly enough and have the right attitude. I don't believe it. We all have weaknesses and limitations as well as strengths. We have to experiment to determine what we *can* do as well as what we *can't* do well. Fritz Perls pointed out that many of us strive to actualize a concept of what we wish to be, rather than to actualize ourselves. We are what we are. It makes no sense to beat yourself for not being able to do something well. As we live and experiment we gradually find our strengths and weaknesses, if we are aware and open to our experiences. Inspiration is wonderful, but if it is not reality-based it is short lived.

* * * * *

We're bound to have variable feelings about ourselves and our performance-in all activities. Feelings generally change pretty fast-depending on one's ongoing thoughts, situations, and the reactions of others. Sometimes, I feel like a damn good therapist. At other times-very ordinary.

* * * * *

Although I see most of the people who come for therapy, if I find that a particular approach is indicated or requested in which I have no training or interest, I refer the person to someone who is more competent in that area. I also refer early in the game if I sense that the person would do better with another therapist (woman, black, older, etc.). Of course, there are therapists who try to narrow the patients' needs down to a few basic, general concepts, and those who believe that a given approach will work for every patient. But, the actual subtle (and not so subtle) variations in expressions of needs and relevant procedures, as they actually occur in therapy, vary greatly. One might say for example, that all a person needs is love, or reinforcement, or insight, or a commitment to a therapeutic situation to really make a behavior change. One can view the task of therapy as being basically simple or complex. I think this depends on the level at which one is discussing therapy- the general underlying factors may be quite simple and basic, but the day to day specifics are complex and varied.

* * * * *

The basic components of psychotherapy are a patient (who's hopefully there to accomplish something), a therapist (with whatever he might have to offer), a room free from distractions, and a reasonably comfortable place for each person to spend some time. Some patients need some tests or apparatus. All the rest is essentially frills and games. You can have the best looking office in town, but shortly after therapy begins, the interaction between the two people becomes dominant. I've talked to therapists who place a high value on fancy addresses, expensive furniture and trimmings, and fashionable clothes, feeling that this impresses the patient, or builds a sense of respect and confidence in the therapist. I think it's fine to have an office that is comfortable for the patient and the therapist, but for most people, I believe that this will have little impact on the effectiveness of therapy. I've heard as many patients comment positively about their progress while in my rather small and barren offices at the hospital and college, as in my better furnished, more spacious office in my home. For some people who have internalized, on the basis of their behavioral histories, a value that impressive offices, fashionable clothes, and high fees equal a more competent therapist, such extras could have an effect on the patient's initial selection of a therapist. I personally like to minimize the stress on frills and focus on the therapy process. I really don't like phonyness.

* * * * *

Just as people enter therapy for many different reasons, and with different expectations, they stop therapy for numerous reasons. Some get what they wanted from a session or two-vent heavy emotions and feel better, reconceptualize their situation, get specific advice, etc. Some stop because they feel they are ready to stop. Some stop because their therapists tell them they are ready. Some, after going for many months or years, arrive at a decision, with their therapists, that they've probably gained as much from therapy as that situation could offer. Some stop because they find it too expensive, or not worth the expense, or have higher priorities as to how to spend their money. Some stop because they feel they are not involved with a good type of therapy, or a compatible therapist, for them. Some stop to escape from, or avoid, uncomfortable feelings which are brought up in therapy. Some stop in order to get involved in a different kind of therapy, or with a different therapist, for good or bad reasons. People stop therapy for many reasons.

* * * * *

Even though the art and science of psychotherapy still have a long way to go, people who do alot of it and care about what they are doing, have an advantage over laymen in dealing with behavioral and emotional problems. By working with many people in therapy, they get ideas of what works and what doesn't work in many situations. For sure, there will still be some therapists who will not be very effective even with alot of experience.

Many laymen are interested in doing mechanical work on their cars, and some get to be very good at it. But, chances are that, in general, the trained mechanic, who spends many hours a day working on a variety of cars, is in a better position to deal with your car troubles than most laymen.

* * * * *

The summer after starting my private practice (about fourteen years ago), I was spending a day at a friends swim club. One of his friends was surprised that I was in practice because I looked so young. He said if he ever went to a therapist he'd want to feel that his therapist had "been through it all." I felt defensive. Like most people, I'd experienced my share of rough times, and I worked hard in graduate school, did alot of reading, had alot of good supervision during my internship, etc. I also believed that I had the basic personal equipment to be a pretty good therapist. I feel, however, that as I have experienced more both in my personal life and in the office, I am, in general, a better therapist now. I've lived through more and have learned alot through trial and error (and trial and success). This does not mean that the quality of therapy correlates directly with the age and experience of the therapist. Obviously there are many other important factors. But,

I believe that despite advances in theory and methodology, the therapist's experience is a very important variable in therapy.

* * * * *

The importance of the temporary nature of feelings brought on by situations is grossly underestimated. So often daily events and situations greatly influence our ongoing feelings. We do well at something, or a number of situations are going nicely, so we feel good. Something unpleasant happens to us, or we find ourselves in uncomfortable situations, and we feel bad. But, often people attribute more permanence to immediate feelings than is realistic. We all experience a gigantic variety of situations-good, bad, in-between, and in response we all experience the full gamut of unpleasant feelings-anxiety, depression, boredom, guilt, anger, etc.-along with the good ones. In therapy, I often point out to the person how the feelings at that moment might be tied to specific ongoing or recent events (or thoughts), or to future expectations. I feel that any school of thought that stresses or promises permanent freedom from unpleasant feelings is not for real. They either try to hypnotize people into focusing only on the good stuff, or encourage a build up of defenses to not feel the effects of many real life situations. This is one of the main faults of many present day (and I'm sure many future) super-duper, quickie approaches which promise permanent happiness and freedom from anxiety and depression. They do something to make you feel good for a while and then say "See, it works." But, then you leave, and you're out in the real world again, with all of its stimuli for bad feelings as well as good ones. The other side of this is that many people who commit suicide do so because they are locked into the idea that the misery they are experiencing will never change. I believe the acceptance of the facts that 1) unpleasant feelings are part of living, and 2) that all feelings are temporary, are important realizations. We are often hit with multiple stimuli-events, people, the words going on in our heads (thoughts)-and our feelings and behavior, at any given time, are the result of the strongest ongoing stimulus, or combination of stimuli.

* * * * *

Often an important part of bringing about a behavior change is tailoring the situation and setting to foster the change, along with the other things being done in therapy. I've recently seen a twenty six year old man who was having an impotence problem. Although he had some sexual experiences resulting in orgasms, most of the time-nothing. After checking matters out physically, he entered therapy. We spent some time exploring early experiences and thoughts that competed with relaxing and enjoying sex spontaneously. We worked on thought-stoppage, a technique in which he shouted "stop" inside his head as soon as he began to think typical thoughts which snowballed, and made orgasm impossible for him. We worked on systematic desensitization of anxiety in sexual situations. As most people who have difficulty in this area, he put alot of pressure on himself, especially during intercourse, to "succeed", and we worked on ways to reduce this self-imposed pressure, and to be more spontaneous. A major factor in this case working out well was tailoring the situation to make him feel more relaxed. In his case it meant-keeping the light off, not drinking too much before sex, not starting unless there was plenty of time ("quickies" made him very nervous), and not starting at too late an hour (when he was very tired). Fortunately, his girlfriend was understanding and agreed to all of these conditions. In dealing with many other kinds of problems, tailoring the situations to maximize the wanted change is also frequently helpful.

* * * * *

Confronting patients with their behavior, defenses, contradictions, and subtle manipulations is generally a valuable tool in therapy. Although confrontation is frequently uncomfortable (for both therapist and patient), it often leads the person to face and deal with important issues, and results in gaining his respect and trust.

* * * * *

So often patients hear what you're saying and act as if they don't care or agree, and then, at a later time, show you that they accepted or acted upon what you had said. We often see this in kids- it seems that they don't want to give their parents the satisfaction of knowing they are listening and being influenced. A therapist can't be sure that because a patient doesn't seem to be accepting something he is saying that it is not having an effect. Sometimes it takes time to evaluate.

* * * * *

Where is the person coming from? What are his thoughts and feelings? What kind of behavior history does he bring to therapy? You can't understand someone's behavior unless you are genuinely interested in such things. A feel for this aspect of the patient is needed, in addition to responding to immediate behavior. In school, students who come to a new unstructured class with a history of very structured learning experiences may feel uncomfortable in the situation, and think that the teacher should be more organized. Other students, coming from a freer, less structured background may have very positive feelings for the same teacher. No teacher or therapist can please all students or patients because they are coming from different places-they've had different experiences, and built in preferences.

* * * * *

Over the years we get conflicting input on so many issues. Should I care what others think of me? Many authors have given the message not to care about the reactions of others, but to look to ourselves for our own evaluations of ourselves and our behavior. In novels and movies we identify with the hero who stands up for his own beliefs and fights the crowd. Fritz Perls talks convincingly about standing on our own feet and using our own eyes and ears. On the other hand, we are given strong messages by parents, teachers, and friends to care about what they have to say about us. In a world where we are in contact with people so much of the time, social influence is a very powerful force. To many personality theorists, the socialization process causes alot of giving up of self, and is the main thing that messes people up. Ideally, we may wish to be sensitive to the thoughts and feelings of other people, and hear their reactions to our behavior and thoughts, but to filter their reactions through our own brains-"Yes, what this person is saying about me makes sense." "No, what that person is saying about me is nonsense." While this is understandable rationally, emotionally it is difficult to put into action. In my experience, while some people are closer than others to this balance of being sensitive to what others are saying, but making their own judgments regarding themselves, I've never seen anyone who was completely there. Most people are too dependent upon the evaluations of others. Many people defensively block out hearing what others are saying about them. A major aspect of people who lack assertiveness is caring too much about the opinions and reactions of others. To work on building one's independence and looking to himself obviously takes alot more than advising the person to be himself. A therapist often has to spend time focusing on, and pushing the person to come into contact with, his real feelings and thoughts about many ongoing situations-both inside and outside of therapy-and has to hold back from too much advice giving or from otherwise giving in to the patient's dependent manipulations. While it may be helpful to give some support for independent thinking, too much support fosters dependence. A therapist's good intentions of being helpful can result in holding the patient back from being independent and self-supporting.

* * * * *

Otto Rank's view of man-as-artist is very appealing to me. I appreciate his emphasis on creativity, individuality, independence, and will. Artists have alot to offer people in showing creative ways to respond to the human condition. In addition to directly experiencing art, reading what great artists have said about their work can be both inspiring and relevant to many aspects of living.

I don't believe that a given period or school of thought in art (e.g. impressionism, expressionism, surrealism, etc.) is more valid or correct than any other. Although one may relate to or appreciate some approaches more than others, each school of thought and each individual artist has something unique to say. Some artists wish to produce the feeling of the scene; some attempt to capture the underlying essence of their subject matter; some look deep within themselves and try to express visually their innermost feelings, thoughts and fantasies; some aim to influence people; some paint or sculpture for themselves, etc. Their intentions and manners of expression vary tremendously.

This relates to individual psychologists, and schools of thought in psychology. Although some positions have much more personal appeal and meaning to me than others, each is looking at behavior in unique ways, and has something to contribute to the whole scheme of things. Being open to the various views can provide a therapist with a richer and more thorough source of ideas for understanding and doing something about changing behavior, than would be possible if one was locked into a more narrow viewpoint.

In therapy sessions, it is so important to recognize, respect, accept, and be responsive to the uniqueness of each individual.

* * * * *

Some patients go from one therapist to the

next looking for magic (and there are always some "therapists" around who promise magic) or to avoid really dealing with their problems. Sometimes if you confront a patient with this and deal with it as an issue it helps. At other times, other factors override your influence on the patient and he continues the pattern. As in the case of other highly resistent patients, it's foolish to take this too personally-unless you enjoy beating yourself.

* * * * *

Does violence on television and in movies make for more violence in people? People often ask psychologists questions like this, and they're often answered on all kinds of levels. "I don't know" is an often true but rare answer to such questions. Pretty nearly everyone has *opinions* about such things (everyone's a psychologist), but some opinions are based on alot more thinking and evidence than others. To give a scientific answer to such a question is very difficult because of all of the variables involved. Statistics on the numbers and percentages of violent acts when compared against population increases have risen. That's a fact. Present day television and movies show more frequent and more vivid violence than in the past. That is also a fact. But, many other changes have also occurred and continue to occur (e.g. changes in child rearing practices, changes in educational philosophies and approaches, changes in many cultural values, changes in the economy, and in the law.) To do meaningful research on such questions requires sorting out the effects of many variables and combinations of variables. To study the effects of violence in movies and television on the incidence of violence in society, probably the most one could expect is to gain some idea of general effects of defined variables on the frequency and nature of violent acts when studying a large number of people. This kind of research cannot predict with certainty whether a given individual will perform violent acts.

On a theoretical level, learning principles might help in making some good guesses about this kind of question. Modeling studies show the effects of viewed violence in a movie on the behavior of children immediately following the movie, but even such research only gives a general trend, and doesn't predict the individual. The child's history of punishment for violent behavior or reward for non-violent behavior, or more powerful modeling of non-violent behavior, or the threat of punishment for such behavior, might well override the impact of the violence in the movie that was observed. Movies and television programs can make violent behavior look appealing or rewarding (excitement, money, getting back at someone, etc.). But, again while this may carry enough weight to encourage some individuals to act violently (if the viewed violence looked rewarding enough, if someone was seriously considering such behavior even before seeing the show, etc.), many other past and present variables will prevent others from acting in this way. Seeing violence in the news can be a stimulus for some to act in a similar way. This may be counterbalanced by seeing others punished for such behavior.

It has been speculated that when people view violence in films and even in contact sports like football and boxing, they vicariously let out aggressive feelings and consequently don't let these feelings out in their daily lives. Again, I believe that many factors in each individual's behavioral history determine whether this happens or not for that person. It seems that this interpretation might be an easy rationalization for those who stand to make alot of money by showing these things to the public. One might also attempt to justify showing violence by indicating that such events are a real part of life, and that by holding back such things, one is censoring the showing of reality.

From a learning viewpoint, it would make sense-theoretically-that if the great majority of television programs and movies modeled non-violent behavior in an appealing way, it would enhance their influence for less violent behavior in the streets. Of course, there would still be all of the other factors that effect violent and non-violent behavior in individuals (e.g. kids in tough neighborhoods will still see alot of violent behavior being rewarded, child rearing practices, direct personal rewards for violent behavior, etc.).

Does violence on television and in movies make for more violence in people? Research and theory can give some ideas, but as simple as this question (and many like it) sounds on the surface, to give a real answer is not easy. Beware of psychologists with ready answers to complex questions.

* * * * *

Some patients try to put you in the position of playing the all-knowing *Answer Man*. It's a good idea to make it clear that this is not the therapist's role.

* * * * *

I have found a working knowledge of theories of learning and behavioral learning concepts to be extremely valuable in the daily practice of therapy.

First, this area provides a very useful model for *understanding* the patient's behavior both in the therapy situation and outside. Second, the psychology of learning offers a tremendous number of alternative *procedures for changing behavior* (motor behavior, verbal behavior, social behavior, thinking, emotions, attitudes, interests, etc.). The Behavior Therapies are practical, therapeutic applications of learning principles. Interest, research, and training in this approach to therapy has grown tremendously during the past twenty years and it is presently one of the major approaches taught in psychology graduate programs in the United States. The appeal of this approach is that the concepts and principles have been arrived at on the basis of rigorous scientific research, and great stress is placed on testing the effectiveness of the various therapy procedures before they are accepted. Behavior Therapies are a reaction to the fact that for many years, hundreds of theoretical approaches to therapy were offered, but were proposed in such a way that they could not be directly tested. As a result, their effectiveness could not be proven or disproven. Therapists tended to accept or reject theories and procedures on the basis of such factors as the eloquence and logical appeal of the theorist, the popularity of the approach, the orientation of their graduate programs and teachers, and the intuitive feel of the approach.

* * * * *

Behavioral learning principles are always operating-even right now (my now and your now) for you and me. For example, my writing is *reinforcing* me for sitting down with the intention of writing, and is an *escape* from less enjoyable things that

I might be doing now-such as writing some reports that will be due shortly. Your reading now may be *reinforcing* for picking up the book, or it may be a *stimulus* for triggering other thoughts, or it may be *punishing* if you're finding it a drag, etc. Although we can isolate the learning concepts and study them in a pure sense, actually many of them are often operating simultaneously in the real world. What we wind up doing is often the product of a combination of factors, and is in response to the factor or factors carrying the most weight at the time.

* * * * *

The range of applicability of learning concepts for changing real, every-day behaviors is tremendous when one has a good understanding of them, and a feeling for their direct use. Many people are initially uncomfortable thinking about their behavior and life situations in this way. In therapy, alot depends on the therapist's understanding of the principles, concepts, and procedures, his ability to see the relevance of a learning model to the behavior change business, and his ingenuity in seeing how particular concepts might be applied to the specific behavior of an individual. They must be applied in relevant and meaningful ways with each person.

Descriptions of basic learning concepts such as reinforcement, punishment, extinction, and modeling, initially give the impression that they are too simplistic or superficial to offer much in the way of understanding or doing something about significant behaviors. During my work as a therapist, however, I have found that the study of this area is relevant and extremely helpful in dealing with a great variety of behaviors (simple and complex), and I hope that during the course of this writing some of this comes through.

* * * * *

Often the effects of various learning studies appear to be obvious, but frequently the obviously expected outcomes don't occur. For example, before discussing studies on punishment, I've often asked students in my theories of learning courses what they predict would happen to an individual's behavior in a specific situation involving punishment. Invariably, I get many different responses. "The behavior will stop." "The behavior will slow down." "The behavior will increase." "Punishment will have no effect." The people tend to use reason, or respond to what they have heard about the effects of punishment from others, or try to look back at their own experiences (often not a bad thing to do). But, studies in this area have shown that if an empirical (effective for the individual) punishment is used, the effects on behavior and the emotional side effects are highly predictable. A great deal of evidence supports the assumption that real learning principles (principles of behavior) have very predictable effects on behavior.

* * * * *

While experimental learning research has little to contribute to some aspects of the therapy situation (for example, the art side-sensitivity, awareness, relationship-deciding what areas to work on with the person), it offers a great deal regarding specific procedures for changing behavior. Of course, in a way, learning relates to nearly everything going on in the therapy session. So much of the personality, interests, attitudes, preferences and emotional responses of both the therapist and the patient are learned during the course of their lives. Similarly, the therapist's basic approach to therapy is strongly related to his past learning experiences-his teachers, books read, things tried before and found to be effective or ineffective.

* * * * *

Before one starts a behavior therapy procedure to change a particular behavior, it is important to do a *behavior analysis,* that is, to view the behavior in its total context (Stimulus-Response-Consequences). *Stimulus* - What kinds of settings and situations or internal thoughts or feelings tend to precede or bring about the particular behavior under focus (target behavior)? *Response* - Specifically what behavior or behaviors occur? *Consequences* - What kinds of consequences follow the behavior-from the environment, other people, within the person himself (thoughts, emotions, physical reactions)? Frequently what appears to be a problematic behavior is telling you something about the person in his situation. The behavior is often understandable, and perhaps quite appropriate, in light of the person's situation.

An example is when one goes into a classroom where children are often noisy with an effective procedure to quiet them down. Before jumping in with such a plan, it's generally a good idea to look at the behavior in its total context. What precedes and follows the noisy behavior? While the approach might be appropriate in some cases, the classes' noisy behavior might be found to be quite understandable when considering the situation in which this behavior occurs-perhaps the teacher is often boring, or unprepared, or goes too fast, or is mean to the kids. The noise may be a very healthy reaction to such a situation. Rather than manipulating the consequences following the children's behavior to quiet them down, in some cases it might be better to focus on some of the teacher's behavior which could be a stimulus for their inattentiveness.

* * * * *

When the goal is to change an uncomfortable feeling such as anxiety or depression, I first try to get a picture of whether the emotion is reactive to a real situation or is more self-imposed, This is part of doing a behavior analysis-looking at the behavior in its total context. In addition to working on gaining understanding of the feeling, I try to make a decision about whether it is better to work on changing some behavior that will result in an accompanying change in the feeling, to work on changing the feeling directly, or both. We could work on activities such as directly desensitizing the anxiety or fear in a given situation, or on stopping specific depressing thoughts which tend to lead to increasingly depressing thoughts. On the other hand, it is often effective to work on changing behavior which results in accompanying changes in feelings.

For example, in working with a person who was very depressed following a stroke which left her partially paralyzed and with a slight speech impairment, we spent considerable time in therapy planning specific activities which would get her out of the house and might spark her interest and enthusiasm-e.g. art classes, travel, volunteer work, card games, night courses. These activities *competed* with her staying home and thinking many depressing thoughts about her losses in ability and limitations in activities. While it was important for her to look at what happened to her realistically, face it, and accept it, working on building specific behaviors which would result in more positive feelings than depression was very effective in this case. Similarly, with students who feel very anxious about taking tests because of insufficient time spent on studying, it would be more appropriate to work on building studying time than to directly desensitize the anxious feelings.

* * * * *

It's a good idea for therapists, to the best of their ability, to constantly keep their eyes and ears open during the therapy situation, with an experimental attitude-Is the present approach working? If not, try something else.
One of the main appeals of Behavior Therapy to me is that it doesn't mystify with mythology, heavy unconscious mentalistic constructs, etc. It's straight forward and practical, and it does not generally take very long to see if what you're doing is having an effect.

* * * * *

If learning principles are real and universal in their applicability to behavior, they should work on covert behaviors as well as overt (observable) behaviors. If I *think* something (a covert behavior-words I am saying to myself) and after I think it I feel good, this feeling can reinforce that thought even though all of this was not observable to another person. Similarly, one might punish a thought or feeling covertly by words he says to himself, or by internal physiological feelings he gets, after the thought or feeling. Although the concepts can only be scientifically studied in observable situations, where they can be measured, they can be operating covertly as well.

* * * * *

The Behavior Therapist, as other therapists, constantly keeps his eyes open and throws out feelers to determine what behavior changes are occurring during therapy. Sometimes, when one undesired behavior is eliminated, other problematic behaviors emerge. At other times when one behavior is improved, several others also improve simultaneously, even though they weren't directly dealt with. The Freudian concept of *symptom substitution* suggests that if you don't get to the root or underlying cause of the problem, and just treat the immediate problematic behavior (the symptom), another problem behavior will emerge because the underlying root cause has not been dealt with.

Although several studies have indicated that symptom substitution often does not occur after a particular behavior has been modified, I have seen cases where it did. A generally agreed upon learning view is that we learn our problem behaviors by the same processes that we learn desired behaviors; therefore, if one learns to change a problem behavior, a new one doesn't necessarily have to emerge. Just as the person *learned* to bite his nails, pick his nose, overeat or smoke, he can *learn* to stop these behaviors. Although this often happens without other unwanted behaviors developing, at times, if the behavior dealt with is just reflecting another more significant ongoing problematic behavior, other problematic behaviors might appear. For example, someone may wish to stop smoking behavior for a variety of reasons-health, expense, disturbing to others, etc. If he began smoking as a result of peer modeling as a teenager, when this person decides to stop this behavior, smoking itself might be the target behavior to be changed directly, and symptom substitution may not occur. In another case, the smoking may be a means of decreasing anxiety resulting from-say-poor communication with a spouse (escape learning). If smoking helps to decrease the person's anxiety level which was caused by the poor communication, decreasing smoking behavior will very possibly result in a new behavior which helps to reduce the anxiety. In this situation, it would make sense to first work directly on improving the poor communication, which is responsible for the tension. Then, if the smoking has not stopped as a result of the general reduction in anxiety, smoking behavior can be dealt with directly.

The difference between this learning-oriented approach and the view of getting to the underlying root cause, is that here we are focusing primarily on situations in the individuals present daily life and recent events, rather than spending a great deal of time delving in detail into the person's past and unconscious processes. In the smoking example, the aim was to deal directly with behaviors which produced the anxiety resulting in smoking, rather than to search the person's past for an understanding of early causes of anxiety, oral needs, etc.

* * * * *

From the standpoint of a learning model, any problem behavior can be learned in many different ways, and similarly, these behaviors can be changed in many ways. This is very different from physical diseases which are often caused by one particular germ, and where the physical cause might only be treated in one way. A person can learn a fear of dogs, for example, by being aware of a parent's fear, seeing someone being bitten or scared by a dog, reading about someone who was hurt by a dog, or by personally having a bad experience with a dog. Although the fear might have been learned by modeling, punishment, classical conditioning, or any one of many other processes, the behavior is essentially the same-fear of dogs. Similarly, this fear might be decreased by means of shaping, reinforcement, fading, classical conditioning, or other approaches. Learning principles offer many ideas when it comes to understanding or going in and doing something about behavior.

* * * * *

Some examples of how behavioral learning concepts help to understand ongoing therapy sessions of any orientation:

Carl Rogers has offered a great deal to the therapist in the way of showing the importance of the relationship, rapport, understanding, honesty, openness, sensitivity, and establishing a good environment for therapy. His client-centered therapy is generally considered a "non-directive" approach in that the intention of the therapist is to function in a way that the patient or client is responsible for changing himself. Rogers was very outspoken against manipulation or control by the therapist. Yet when taped therapy sessions with Rogers and a variety of clients were viewed from the standpoint of learning principles, it was seen that even a therapist who was being very careful not to manipulate or direct was subtly (although not intentionally) doing so. When Rogers was quiet or less responsive (extinction-withholding reinforcement) the patient tended to speak less about the particular content area. When Rogers either reflected the patient's feelings (an important part of his therapy) or even emitted "mmhmmm's", these responses served to reinforce the patient for continuing to talk about the same content areas. An awareness of this simple *verbal conditioning* process could be important to the therapist. Apparently even a therapist's attention, simple verbalizations, and quiet periods have a considerable effect on such patient behaviors as staying on a given topic, dealing with more or less important topics, avoiding, engaging in defensive talk, etc.

Studies have indicated the effects of *modeling* in therapy sessions. Whether the therapist is aware of it or not, parts of his behavior are frequently being picked up by the patient by means of modeling-verbal behavior, values, attitudes, etc. Rogers' patients tend to incorporate careful listening, attentiveness to feelings, being supportive and understanding in this way. Fritz Perls' patients might have incorporated his stress on being direct, calling attention to ongoing responses in other people they were relating to, cursing more, etc. Psychoanalytic patients may become more analytical when relating to others, speak more about ongoing fantasies, underlying motivations, etc., at least in some measure, because of modeling after their therapists.

The relaxing atmosphere in many therapists' offices, and the therapists' calm manner while hearing people speak about situations that are upsetting them greatly, probably enhance new associations for the patient while thinking and talking about these situations (*classical condition-*

ing).
The point in these examples is that an understanding of learning principles can help the therapist to become aware of some of the intentional and unintentional influences going on during any kind of therapy session. Since these influences exist, an awareness of them may be used to simply add to the therapist's understanding of what is happening during the session, or may be used to facilitate the therapy.

* * * * *

To use Behavior Therapy procedures one need not come across as a cold, impersonal machine. In fact, using even the best of methods in this manner, the outcome would most likely be less effective, if not totally ineffective. I believe that it is generally important for the patient to sense that the therapist is genuinely involved and caring if the treatment is to be successful. When starting my research at New York University Medical Center, geared to improve the speech of aphasics by means of applying behavioral learning principles, my aim was to produce rigorous, clean research which would hopefully be effective and practical. I put so much energy into careful measurement and control that I neglected responding to the person behind the various response classes and numbers. Several patients who sensed this, withdrew from the project after very few sessions. Once I began to spend some time just talking to the people, prior to and following the treatment procedure, there was almost no drop-out rate, and the therapy generally went quite smoothly. I had to establish myself as a reinforcer before the experimental therapy could be effective. A great deal of the early literature in the Behavior Therapies was a real turn-off to many humanistically oriented therapists because of its emphases on science and techniques. But, it is not inscribed on a tablet that one cannot include specific procedures, when it is believed they might be helpful, along with a general caring, understanding, humanistic approach to patients.

It is my impression that while learning concepts are relevant and very valuable in *understanding* a great deal of what is going on in therapy, the *application* of specific learning concepts comes into play when procedures are needed to bring about particular, agreed upon (with the patient) changes in the patient's behavior. Such procedures may be systematically used a great deal, a little, or not at all during the course of therapy, depending upon the perceived needs of the patient.

* * * * *

SOME PATIENTS

The following are brief sketches of some people I have seen in therapy during the past few years-their stated problems, their apparent needs (as I perceived them), and some things we did in therapy. The aim of this section is to give an idea of the range of people seen in a general suburban practice, the great variety of needs and stated problems presented in therapy, and the tremendous range of therapeutic approaches and skills called for. In each case we tried to gain *understanding* of the situation, and decided upon *things to do*, hopefully, to improve matters. To encounter all of these individuals with a single theoretical approach, or a narrow idea of what is called for in *all* situations would have been of limited value to many of the people cited even in this small sample.

* * * * *

PATIENT ONE - MIKE

DESCRIPTION

Thirty three year old male, very intelligent, sensitive, egocentric. Came from low income family, but by the time he was in his mid twenties, developed a business in the applied arts which gave him an annual income in the hundreds of thousands of dollars. He lived extravagantly. Very outgoing, dynamic personality.

PROBLEM

Highly anxious for years, but since his separation from his wife, Mike was overwhelmed with anxiety to the point of feeling almost incapacitated at work and in his daily activities. His anxiety seemed to be due to his feelings about separation, feelings of educational inadequacy since he never went to college, a lack of acceptance of any personal weaknesses, and a feeling of searching for meaning in his life. Although Mike was very successful in a monetary and business sense at an early age, he was becoming disinterested and bored with his work, and expressed his feeling of "working so hard for this and now that I'm here something's missing."

APPARENT NEEDS IN THERAPY

Decrease anxiety level. Think through what he wishes to do regarding his marriage, further education, work. Deal with his resentment and lack of acceptance of any personal weaknesses. Understand and deal with the issue of what would give him a greater sense of meaningfulness in his life.

APPROACHES

Discussed specific things Mike could do to decrease his anxiety level (e.g. living more in here-now and accepting all parts of himself), worked on systematic desensitization of anxiety in situations that produced most anxiety, explored pros and cons of reconciliation with his wife in more detail than he'd done in the past (and tried to look at the conflict more objectively). Thoroughly discussed good points and bad points of continuing in his present line of work. Worked on helping Mike to accept himself as he is (weaknesses as well as strengths). Therapy with Mike lasted approximately one year, on a weekly basis. His anxiety level was reduced within the first four sessions with behavior therapy and Gestalt therapy procedures, and because he had a chance to ventilate strong feelings. During the course of therapy he and his wife accepted their decision that a divorce was best for both of them. He decided to continue in his business while engaging in some of the interests he had long wished to pursue outside of his work- flying lessons, photography and enrolling in several evening college courses that appealed to him. He gradually came to accept personal limitations along with his strengths.

PATIENT TWO - ANNE

DESCRIPTION

Twenty nine year old unmarried female, intelligent, very quiet and withdrawn, still living with parents who had always put her down. Held a bookkeeping job in small company since graduating high school. Taking one or two evening college courses each term. No other outside interests. Seldom left house after work. Overweight, neatly dressed. Depressed expression and posture. Looked down alot, infrequent eye contact.

PROBLEM

Felt very anxious in nearly all interpersonal situations, and depressed about herself and her life. Anne believed nothing ever worked out well for her. She hated and was terrified of catholic school as a child. Disliked her work, although it was one of the few places she felt some sense of security, stability and belongingness. She had a habit of sabotaging anything that began to give her some hope for her future. She feared taking tests in college and participating in class discussions, and was thinking of dropping out although she felt college offered a chance for improving her life. Anne always had a goal and fantasy of marriage although she was afraid of men, and avoided them. She was thinking of suicide although she was afraid to carry it out.

APPARENT NEEDS IN THERAPY

Decrease anxiety level and feelings of helplessness and depression. Improve self-concept and gain insight into her self-defeating behavior pattern. Take realistic steps toward and follow through with plans for improving her life in the areas that particularly upset her (i.e. interpersonal relationships, developing relationships with men, seeking outside interests, determining and moving toward a vocation that interested her). Change attitude of hopelessness and meaninglessness.

APPROACHES

Gave Anne the opportunity to make contact with another human being (me), and form a meaningful relationship. Systematic desensitization of anxiety in major areas that disturbed her. Role played speaking to teachers, bosses, her father, and other men, to practice behavior that she had never developed. Discussed pros and cons of various approaches to meeting men and establishing relationships with them. Discussed pros and cons of various jobs that interested her and steps toward making a change. Discussed advantages and difficulties relating to moving out of her parents home and into her own apartment. Reinforced any efforts made to take responsibility for and do something about her situation. Expressed understanding of Anne's deeply unhappy feelings. Gave a great deal of emotional support. I think it was also helpful for her to see that despite our facing and exploring her most distressing feelings, I was not knocked out by them and maintained a sense of humor.

Anne was in therapy for a year and a half, at first on a weekly basis, then, for the last half year, every other week. During the course of therapy; she moved into her own apartment; changed jobs to an office which she found more enjoyable; began taking lessons in flower arranging, sewing, and dancing; started attending outing club and discussion group meetings for singles; and developed friendships with a few women. She came to feel increasing confidence in her ability to do something about her situation. Although Anne is still periodically upset that she has not formed a close relationship with a man, she is more comfortable with men and she is no longer experiencing the helplessness or desperation that she had felt.

* * * * *

I am feeling some frustration in writing these sketches because I am aware that to do justice to any one of the individuals would require much more space. Each one is really a book in himself. I am just trying to capture a bit of the essence of each person, to give a feeling for their situations and individual needs in therapy.

* * * * *

PATIENT THREE - LENNY

DESCRIPTION

Thirty four year old male, separated from his wife and children, intelligent, hard working, good looking, amiable personality. Very high achiever all his life. Superintendent of schools in a prosperous community. Lived comfortably. Enjoyed his work.

PROBLEM

Strong sense of responsibility, for doing the right thing and doing it well, and felt pressured by the demands he placed on himself. Put alot of energy into appearing relaxed, happy, and on top of everything. Very distressed about coming to terms with his central conflict-whether to return to his wife and children because he felt he *should* and was feeling alot of guilt along these lines, or get involved more with (perhaps marry) another woman whom he had met and felt very close to. Not an infrequent modern dilemma. Severe headaches. Feelings of tension which interfered with functioning at work.

APPARENT NEEDS IN THERAPY

Come to a conclusion regarding his conflict, and follow through with his decision. Gain understanding of where his "should's" were coming from. Ease up on his frequently self-imposed pressures. Come into better contact with his real feelings and accept them as part of himself.

APPROACHES

Gave Lenny a safe place to spill his guts out about every aspect of the conflict situation. Discusses his parents' great expectations of him since early childhood. Objectively discussed the pros and cons of returning to his family, building his relationship with the other woman, and remaining unattached and uncommitted for awhile. Worked on relaxation exercises which he could practice. Had Lenny roleplay the two opposing sides of his thinking-the side that said "go home" and the side that said "leave for good." In this Gestalt therapy procedure, each side of his thinking directly confronted and responded to the other side verbally.

Lenny's therapy lasted three months, on a weekly basis. His anxiety and headaches were greatly relieved within a month. He decided to return to his wife and children and end his relationship with the other woman. After an initial period of being upset over the loss of this woman, Lenny became increasingly comfortable with his decision.

PATIENT FOUR - GARY

DESCRIPTION

Forty two year old married male, intelligent, very verbal, witty. For about a year Gary held a position as a chemical engineer, but had a history of frequent job changes after rapidly becoming disenchanted with each. Dressed in a carefree manner and did not appear particularly anxious or depressed. Came to therapy primarily because his wife, who feared therapy herself, felt it would help him in matters that she felt were wrong with him (i.e. his sloppiness, teasing her, unpolished manner in groups, etc.). He had never considered leaving his wife, but since she hinted that if he did not enter therapy she would probably leave, he thought he'd see what it was all about. Gary brought a package of little problems to each session initially, to have something to talk about. Although he did not completely avoid discussing things I brought up, he tended to talk about them superficially, and I frequently felt that he was not really listening to, or processing things that were going on in the session. Gary frequently resorted to humor (often good) to avoid heavy feelings or getting into substantial issues.

PROBLEM

Gary said he wished to change his sloppiness, teasing and other behaviors that disturbed his wife. Although he didn't say that he wanted to change jobs again soon, he complained a great deal about his boss, the inefficiency of the company, other employees, etc., and he indicated that he aimed to obtain a higher position in the company. He seemed to use a lack of commitment and identification with his work as a defense, to aid in not getting more angry and upset about his situation. Gary periodically brought in problems he was having with his children, generally centering around poor communication.

APPARENT NEEDS IN THERAPY

To explore Gary's real reasons for coming to therapy. To change some of his attitudes and behavior if it was meaningful for him to do so. Explore his relationship with his wife. To get in better touch with his feelings about himself, his wife and children, his work, and other people and events. To gain insight into his use of humor, lack of real involvement and caring about work, and other defenses.

APPROACHES

Gary came to me because he knew that I taught and practiced behavior modification, and he saw his main problem as simply changing some behaviors that disturbed his wife. This approach appealed to the "engineer" in him. Before jumping in with techniques, we explored how *he* felt about changing the behaviors that he was *sent* to change, and discussed how he felt about therapy-did he really want to be there? Our discussions re-conceptualized his ideas about what he was doing there, and what *he* really wished to do. His use of humor as a defense was pointed out, every time he used it to ease his anxiety or get away from an issue. (Some people who resist therapy just sit there, or don't come, or come late; others escape or avoid with humor, tangents, etc.). After the first few sessions, we talked at length about Gary's real feelings concerning many areas of his life, and I did alot of reflecting of his feelings as I perceived them. We didn't use any formal behavior modification plan during our sessions.

Therapy with Gary lasted approximately six months-once a week. The major outcomes of therapy were his increased awareness and acceptance of himself, increased communication and assertiveness with his wife and children, and putting more caring and energy into his work. Although Gary's increased openness and assertiveness led to some heated confrontations with his wife, they both said that their relationship had improved.

PATIENT FIVE - KAREN

DESCRIPTION

A fifty four year old married woman, with

three grown children, attractive, very depressed. Karen had a stroke which resulted in brain damage in the left cerebral hemisphere causing permanent paralysis of her right arm, partial paralysis of her right leg, slight receptive aphasia (some difficulty in understanding things said to her and written material), slight to moderate expressive aphasia (difficulty in expressing herself verbally). She entered therapy about a year and a half after her stroke. Prior to this condition, Karen was a very active housewife with many outside interests and activities in the community. She had learned to walk slowly with a leg brace and a cane, and was going to a Rehabilitation Center three times a week to learn how to do more things for herself. Although she was reportedly very outgoing before her stroke, afterwards she avoided most situations that involved socializing, or even coming into contact with people.

PROBLEM

Karen was very depressed about her condition and was not sure that she wished to live. Although she hoped her functioning would improve greatly, she was told by her physicians that while physical therapy and speech therapy would help somewhat, total or near total recovery was very unlikely. (It is impossible to give a specific picture of the extent of recovery following a stroke because it depends on so many factors-i.e. the extent of and specific areas of the brain effected, nature of the therapy, committment of patient to exercising and following the therapy plan, extent that weakened brain cells recover, etc.). Although Karen went to therapy classes, she was frequently not motivated to work hard. She was very self-conscious about her appearance and poor verbal skills and being with other people made her anxious and withdrawn. She resented the condescending, overly sympathetic and "helpful" attitude of people when she was with them. Her self-image, which had always been excellent, was now very poor.

APPARENT NEEDS IN THERAPY

To increase acceptance of herself, as she was, while at the same time being motivated to do all she could to improve her functioning. Decrease interpersonal anxiety and extreme depression, and increase her sense that life is still worth living. Seeking and taking steps toward new interests and activities within the realm of her capabilities, and rekindling sparks of interest in previous activities which she gave up on but was still capable of doing. Building self-concept. Increase independent behaviors, and entering programs which might help in this direction.

APPROACHES

Systematic desensitization of anxiety in situations that she avoided. Role-played speaking in various situations (e.g. ordering in a restaurant, buying things in various kinds of stores, answering the phone, etc.). Set up and worked on reinforcement program for improving conversational speech. (I had done research in this area at the Institute of Rehabilitation Medicine, New York University Medical Center). Gave Karen's husband a home program to work on each day-to improve her speech. Encouraged her to take special driving lessons for people with her problem-to allow her more freedom to get around. Showed understanding of her very depressed feelings, but reassured her that she could take responsibility for doing specific things to improve her situation, even if her physical condition did not improve. Encouraged taking painting classes and attending music lectures, which she had wished to do for years, and when she began these activities, gave a great deal of support for following through. Gave her the chance to let out her feelings without giving phoney pep-talks. Discussed the differences between a reactive depression (to a real misfortune) and a self-imposed depression. Told her, honestly, that with people who were essentially okay emotionally before a stroke, after a period of depression, feelings generally improved even without psychotherapy (once the situation was truly faced and accepted). Did all I could to show Karen that she was still a person worthy of respect and caring. Had periodic sessions with her and her husband to work on improving their communication and increasing his awareness of her thoughts and feelings.

Karen was in therapy for eight months-once a week for the first six months, then once every two weeks. She became increasingly accepting of her condition, and at the same time, became motivated to work harder on her physical rehabilitation program. As she participated in more activities and pushed herself to be more active socially, her confidence and self-image improved markedly.

PATIENT SIX - MARY

DESCRIPTION

Nineteen year old, pleasant, attractive, socially immature, shy, self-conscious, rather anxious appearing female. Severe stutterer since five years old (a common age for such behavior to begin). Had a couple of close friends, but often avoided people. In addition to years of speech therapy in and outside of school, Mary's parents had taken her to two psychiatrists within the past few years, and she had gone to each for approximately six months. She said that the psychiatrists spent alot of time trying to find the underlying causes of her stuttering, and she didn't feel it was helping. She was a good student in elementary school and an average student in high school, even though she never participated in classroom discussions unless she absolutely had to. She did her homework and class assignments conscienciously. Came from a religious Catholic family. Mary's father was a very strong, dominant figure in the family, and her mother was quiet, but supportive. She had never stood up to her father when she disagreed with him or was not permitted to do something she wished to do. She held her anger in and sometimes rebelled passively (e.g. did poorly in some schoolwork in which her father wanted her to do particularly well, became quieter in situations where her father told her to speak up, etc.). Her father, meaning well, gave her frequent pep-talks to encourage her to be more outgoing, but she felt submissive and helpless in his presence. He listened very little to her words and feelings. Mary hoped to find work as a secretary, but was afraid to go for interviews although her typing, clerical, and stenographic skills were good.

PROBLEM

Wished to stop stuttering so she would feel more comfortable with people, make more friends, and feel better about looking for a job.

APPARENT NEEDS IN THERAPY

Increase self-acceptance regardless of what happened with her speech. Decrease stuttering. Improve self-image and self-confidence, and stop her from putting herself down so frequently. Decrease anxiety in relating to people. Build assertiveness and expression of thoughts and feelings, particularly with authority figures (father, teachers, bosses). Come into better contact with her real feelings-particularly to gain awareness of when she is feeling negative emotions (e.g. anger, anxiety, depression) and acceptance that it's alright and not crazy to feel such things. To gain insight into her earlier and present relationship with her father, and to see how this relationship related to her behavior. To plan and follow through with steps toward gaining independence, and to start acting on her wish to find a job.

APPROACHES

The sessions were spent on gaining insight into Mary's situation, and on changing behaviors related to her personal life and stuttering. Encouraged and reinforced assertive behavior during the session. Reinforced when she spoke of specific incidences of more open and assertive behavior which occurred during the week. Discussed specific behaviors involved in meeting new people, obtaining a job, etc. Gave emotional support for activities she did well. Encouraged her not to focus as much on the act of speaking (muscle control, breathing, specific sounds) or on how others might be reacting to her, but to focus more on the situation or people she was responding to and on *what she was saying*. Discussed the thoughts in Mary's head as she was speaking, and showed how they might be interfering. Briefly discussed how, on the basis of things she remembered from early childhood, her fear of confronting her father interfered with expressing herself. Discussed her particular secondary gains (reinforcers) for stuttering (e.g.-she felt shy about speaking out, and by stuttering, her teachers would seldom call on her for fear of embarrasing her; it gained sympathy and more gentle behavior from her father and others, etc.). Role played on the phone-I called my office on the intercom from another room, and she answered the telephone as if doing so for a company (she had always felt very uncomfortable about answering phones); then I reinforced when she did it well. Systematic desensitization of anxiety in situations which particularly effected Mary's speech. Used an escape conditioning procedure that Israel Goldiamond found to be effective with many stutterers (constant tone when stuttering while reading-tone off during all periods of fluency). Worked on a specific reinforcement procedure, counting number of words and disfluencies for one minute time samples, and systematically reinforced better and better speech.

At the end of therapy, about one year later, Mary's stuttering decreased considerable. Behavior therapy, client-centered therapy, supportive therapy, and insight therapy procedures all contributed to her improvement. She is presently enjoying and functioning well in her work, as secretary in a large insurance company, and is happier in her personal life.

PATIENT SEVEN - LYNN

DESCRIPTION

Twenty six year old, pleasant, quiet, attractive, subtly sexy and flirtatious married woman. Married five years, three children. No real hobbies or outside interests. Worked as medical secretary before marriage. Appeared shy, but covered feelings of anxiety and depression from herself and others. Did some drinking nearly every day.

PROBLEM

Lynn stated that she sought therapy mainly because she didn't enjoy sex, and it upset her and her husband that she never had an orgasm. She had believed from the start of her marriage that she didn't love her husband, although she respected his intelligence and abilities. Lynn was afraid of his temper because he hit her on several occasions-the first time on their honeymoon. She thought he was perverted in his feelings about sex, and felt that when they were involved in sex he thought only of his own pleasure. She said although she didn't like it, he would often tie her up with her stockings, and insist that she wear a particular garter while they were having intercourse. (Fine with me, if they were *both* into it that way.) She felt obligated to have sex with him although she was never very attracted to him sexually. Lynn found that the realities of marriage and having children were nothing like her early fantasies of what it was going to be like. She was depressed, disillusioned and very down on herself, and she saw no way out. She felt guilty about the prospect of leaving because of the children, and because she felt she couldn't make it on her own. Lynn didn't think it would be fair to her children if she found a job, and she lacked confidence in her ability to hold a job.

APPARENT NEEDS IN THERAPY

Clarify real feelings about husband, marriage, children, sex. Determine what Lynn wanted to do with her life-(e.g. remain married or separate; find a job or not). If she decided that she really wanted to improve matters sexually, work out some specific things she and her husband might do differently (if clearer insight into the situation or a change in attitude was not sufficient in itself-which it is often not). Build self-image, and feelings of competence, decrease anxiety concerning sex and interpersonal relationships. Find interests and activities to make her life more meaningful and enjoyable. Decrease Lynn's excessive drinking.

APPROACHES

Discussed in detail various areas in which Lynn experienced confused and conflicting feelings. Encouraged her to continue thinking about these issues beyond the point where it became uncomfortable, and showed her how she tended to escape from staying with uncomfortable thoughts until they were worked through (e.g. by putting herself down, drinking, giving up, etc.). Discussed Lynn's dreams, in which her husband was totally overwhelming her and making her feel like "a nothing", and had her role play the various parts of the dreams to clarify her feelings, and gain a better understanding of each part of her conflicts. Reinforced her for persevering toward thinking uncomfortable problems through, and for taking steps to make her situation better. Gave support for things she did well. Brought out into the open and honestly discussed her feelings about me, when it became clear that she wanted a romantic relationship, and explained where I believed the feelings were coming from-(Lynn was responding to an understanding, supportive, attentive male who was talking to her about her most private feelings. It appeared to be these behaviors in me, in this situation, that brought about her feelings-"Interpreted the transference", psychoanalysts would say.) Systematic desensitization of anxiety in sexual activities. Thought stoppage -suggested that as soon as she began to pressure herself to reach an orgasm and to criticize herself for not feeling what she "should" feel to shout "Stop!" in her head, and bring herself to the ongoing situation, or to a fantasy which would enhance the sexual contact. Discussed some specific thoughts with Lynn and her husband to tailor the situation to maximize the sexual enjoyment of both.

During the course of therapy, which lasted about ten months, Lynn decided to leave her husband. She concluded that she did not really love him, and probably married him for the wrong reasons. She is presently adjusting to her new life -a job in promotions with a department store, and a relationship with a man she has been dating for about a half year. In this relationship she is communicating more openly and is enjoying sex very much.

PATIENT EIGHT - BARRY

DESCRIPTION

Thirty three year old outgoing, hard-working, unmarried man. Living in an apartment with thirty eight year old brother who was dying of cirrhosis of the liver. Father died when he was ten years old, and then Barry lived with his mother-a strong willed, dominating woman-until she had died, three years prior to his entering therapy. Bearded, dressed modestly, spoke in colorful, earthy way. Didn't appear overly depressed or anxious. Enjoyed his work as a machinist for a company he had been with for more than five years.

PROBLEM

Found my name in the phonebook, and said on the phone that he wished to start therapy to cut down on his drinking. During the first session, Barry said that he and his brother drank a great deal, and that his brother recently learned that he had an advanced case of cirrhosis of the liver. Barry then told me about his own uncontrollable aggressive behavior when he was drunk. In the most severe and most recent example, he was charged with "atrocious assault and battery", for badly beating his girlfriend after seeing her at a bar with her ex-boyfriend. When she left the bar and returned to her cottage, Barry humiliated her verbally, and beat her to the point of breaking her nose and several ribs. After she managed to escape from him, he burned down her cottage. On other past occasions, he also resorted to alcohol to free himself from any inhibitions to act aggressively. Once he was sober he felt ashamed and guilty, and swore he would never repeat such behavior. But, he knew that in the past these promises were always overridden by immediate responses to events that riled him. Barry felt it was time to take some action to control his drinking and his temper. He was also concerned about his self-centeredness, and his jealousy regarding his girlfriend.

APPARENT NEEDS IN THERAPY

Gain understanding and control of temper and drinking. Deal with frustrating situations by facing them and thinking them through rather than giving himself an excuse to act wildly. Gain understanding and control of his feelings of jealousy. Build communication skills and tendency to use them when he felt angry or frustrated. Build sensitivity and awareness of other people's needs. Clarify his personal goals-Did he want a permanent relationship with a woman? How did he wish to live? Build his self-concept and sense of independence.

APPROACHES

Discussed specifics of various past events which led to using drinking as an excuse to act aggressively-to build insight into this behavior pattern. Set up behavior modification plan for self-reinforcement of non-drinking behavior and self-punishment of drinking behavior. Strongly reinforced when he avoided drinking, and called attention to and reinforced his sense of satisfaction when he exercised self control. Explored Barry's feelings about drinking and how he coped on days that he remained sober. Discussed in detail his thoughts and feelings about his girlfriend, and the nature of their relationship. Explored future goals. Worked on staying with negative, uncomfortable feelings when they arose-living with them, accepting them as part of living, and thinking in terms of productive ways to act on them. Spent some time exploring the origins of Barry's feelings of lack of control and of aggressiveness. Kept the atmosphere as relaxed as possible while discussing very anxiety-provoking subjects.

Therapy lasted one year-two times a week during the first few months, once a week for the next few months, and then, once every two weeks until termination. During therapy, there were several occasions when he did some drinking, but for the last five months he didn't drink. Barry came to understand his anger better, and learned to release anger more constructively, and to delay his tendency to respond impulsively. At the end of therapy, he was feeling more comfortable with himself.

PATIENT NINE - GRETA

DESCRIPTION

Thirty three year old, slightly overweight, artily dressed, straggly haired, woman, with very lively expressions and gestures. Enjoyed and participated in the arts since childhood. Was married to an artist (painter) for six years before divorce, and was living with another painter for approximately three years when she entered therapy. Greta was a competent potter and sculptress, and taught crafts privately.

PROBLEM

After her van was totaled by a large truck, two years before entering therapy, Greta had much less energy, poor endurance, and daily pain in her back and neck. She felt depressed and frustrated by her loss of ability to work long hours on her crafts. She had previously worked ten hours a day. In addition to her practical concern about loss of income, she was primarily upset about what she perceived as a loss of her creative urge and creative ability. Greta felt that her pieces looked stiffer and lacked the originality of her previous work. Since her accident, she was only able to work an hour or two each day, and her attention to her physical condition was greatly overriding her concentration on work activities. She wished to recapture her creative abilities and to increase productivity.

APPARENT NEEDS IN THERAPY

Determine whether Greta's decrease in work activity and feeling of lost creativity were really due mainly to her physical condition, or whether psychological factors also played a significant part. Determine whether she was doing all she could to improve her physical problems and if not, to explore why, and encourage her to do so. Assess whether she had truly lost a great deal of her ability to think creatively, and deal with her feelings about this important area of her life. Increase hours working on crafts if possible, or if she was unable to do so, explore feasible alternatives. Build self-image, since this was getting increasingly poor since her productivity had decreased.

APPROACHES

Worked on building trust and confidence in me, since Greta had an underlying general distrust of 'doctors'-briefly discussing some of my interests and activities in the arts, expressing my concern over her particular dilemma, and attempting to help her to see that I was a *for real* person besides being a 'doctor'. Discussed her secondary gains for not working, and explored whether she might be using her physical condition to avoid work. Discussed Greta's present rehabilitation program, and suggested some centers that might offer more in the way of treatment. Administered several tests to particularly assess intelligence, possible neurological impairment, and creative functioning (e.g. the Wechsler Adult Intelligence Scale, Bender-Gestalt, Rorschach), and gave her detailed feedback on the test findings. The outcome of testing indicated that she was functioning at a very high intellectual level; no significant neurological or perceptual-motor deficits were suggested; and her responses to the projective (personality) test were unusually creative. This 'objective' information was very reassuring to her and helped to lessen her fears and concerns in these areas. Set up a behavior modification plan to gradually increase Greta's daily working hours over a period of several months (prior to therapy she viewed working as an all or none activity). We discussed progress in this area on a regular basis. The intention was that by pushing the desired behavior, in this situation, it would improve Greta's feelings about herself, and would show her that some of her imagined fears were not real.

Greta was in therapy for a year and a half-on a weekly basis for a year, then once every two or three weeks. She began to pace herself better, and gradually worked up to seven or eight hours a day on her sculpting and pottery. Once she was more confident about her creativity and productivity, our sessions focused increasingly on other areas that concerned her-such as her difficulties in forming long term relationships with men.

PATIENT TEN - JOHN

DESCRIPTION

Fifty three year old, youthful, slim, well dressed, outgoing, married man with four children. Received bachelors and masters degrees in business at ivy league colleges. Earned very high salary as vice-president of a large corporation. Married at thirty to a woman who was working successfully in her profession. History of high ambition and high achievement at school and work. Enjoyed his position, and was good at his work. Strong interests in the arts and participating in sports-golf, tennis, jogging. Appeared relaxed, successful, on top of things.

PROBLEM

Miserable at home, although he spoke highly about his wife's intelligence, appearance, accomplishments, abilities as a homemaker and mother. John kept a detailed notebook to support his suspicion that his wife was "cheating" on him, and he was obsessed with jealousy and anger at her. He stated that while he didn't love her, he respected her in many ways and felt it would be foolish to leave her. He had poor relationships with all of his children (ranging in age from twelve to twenty one). His wife was "in charge of raising the children", and he had little involvement with them. At work, John was "crazy over" one of the secretaries, a twenty seven year old woman; and while he flirted with her and took her to lunch occasionally, she had no interest in forming a closer relationship. He couldn't understand how in this day and age she wouldn't be interested in him sexually, or in going out with him, expecially since he could offer her a great deal in terms of promotions and raises. He was in conflict as to whether or not he should separate from his wife. He had difficulty in accepting his age. He wanted advice as to how to make the secretary become more interested in him. He was also concerned about his excessive smoking (three packs a day) and drinking (one pint a day), and he wished to cut down on these habits.

APPARENT NEEDS IN THERAPY

Gain clarification of who he is and what he wants from life. Work through John's conflict about remaining with his family or leaving (despite his success in many areas, he lacked confidence in living on his own). Determine his real feelings about his relationship with the secretary-was it the actual person, or other factors in the relationship with a young, attractive woman that appealed to him? Clarify whether or not John should pursue intimate relationships with females outside of marriage-given his values and goals. Gain understanding of roles he was playing. Improve contact with his honest feelings. Determine the causes of his jealousy, and deal with this issue. Decrease smoking and drinking.

APPROACHES

Gave close, direct feedback on his behavior and roles he played during therapy-e.g. when he was avoiding, boasting, trying to make me like him, lying, etc. Discussed roles John played in many situations, and explored the intentions and consequences of these roles. Frequently questioned his real feelings about issues discussed, and confronted him when his facial expression, posture, voice quality, etc. led me to question his words. Discussed thoughts and feelings for and against remaining with his family. Discussed his pros and cons for forming a closer relationship with the secretary, or with other women. Explored John's fantasies about younger women. Had him role play and identify with two sides of himself-the side which told him what he *wanted* to do, and the part which told him what he *should* do. The overt expression of these two sides, and the confrontation of each side with the other, clarified the conflict and helped somewhat. Discussed short term and long term personal goals. Explored his jealous feelings, possible causes for these feelings, and discussed a variety of ways for dealing with and overcoming them. Discussed John's excessive drinking and smoking, and how he used these things to cover up or escape from his uncomfortable feelings; and set up a behavior modification plan for decreasing these habits.

During the three months that John remained in therapy, he showed variable motivation and commitment to working on and dealing with his situation. He frequently sabotaged our efforts, broke appointments, and went on many tangents during our sessions. His smoking and drinking habits went up and down during these months, and he did not resolve his conflict regarding his family and secretary when he chose to terminate therapy. At the end of therapy, he stated that he thought therapy would work faster. Working with John was quite frustrating at times.

* * * * *

These sketches were presented to give a small sample of the great variety of individuals, problems, therapeutic needs, and approaches called for in a general therapy practice. They didn't begin to do justice to the richness of the lives of the people or of the therapy sessions, and this sample didn't touch upon an infinite variety of other situations. Not one child was discussed. So many things are happening during each session relating to the relationship, the problem at hand, the state of mind of the patient and therapist at that time, and so forth. As much as the therapist tries to be all there and aware of as much as possible during the session, there are always other things happening, for better or for worse, at the same time. All you can do as therapist is to be all you can at that time and to do your job as well as possible. Be all you can in terms of intuition, sensitivity, awareness and understanding, as well as in knowing and using relevant theory and procedures.

In each case, I assessed the situation as well as I could, and tried to do meaningful and effective things in therapy. As you read the sketches, you might have been impressed by other apparent needs, and might have been inclined to approach the situations in other ways. The possible directions to go, and approaches to employ, are infinite. The main point is that in the actual practice of therapy there is no single way to meet the needs of all of the people who come into therapy-unless you deal with very specific problems, in a very narrow, selected range of patients. In a general psychotherapy practice, I believe that therapy should center on the patient's individual needs, and that an open, eclectic approach is generally the most practical and helpful.

A FINAL NOTE

In the process of writing this book, I discovered that ideas for more and more notes keep coming, and I find in rereading them that some thoughts and impressions change somewhat over time. It is certainly not a complete or unchanging summary of my thoughts and feelings about therapy.

I hope it came across that, despite my criticisms, I have great feelings for psychology, and respect both humanistic and scientific contributions to therapy. I believe that an understanding and appreciation of both areas, the art and science of therapy, is important in this field. Either side alone doesn't meet the total needs of most people who enter therapy. Stressing the significance of the relationship, sensitivity, awareness, caring, honesty, understanding, and acceptance are as important as knowing something about the science and technology of bringing about behavior changes.

I enjoyed working on the notes that comprise this book. It was a pleasure to just write what came, without pushing things into a rigid format. Sitting down and writing about the various areas helped me to think through some issues and clarify some of my own thinking. I would like to encourage other practicing therapists to keep notes of their thoughts, impressions, and personal experiences, for their own clarification and to share with others. I for one, would be interested in sharing and learning from such writings.

* * * * *

I would be very interested in hearing your reactions to this book, if you should care to write.

                Bob Goodkin
                Department of Psychology
                Montclair State College
                Upper Montclair, New Jersey 07043

SOME BOOKS

The following are a sample of books which I have found to be valuable and relevant to my work as a therapist. Some relate to the underlying philosophy. Some relate to the science and procedures. Some relate to the art, or craft. Some of the books listed are from areas that initially appear to be far afield from psychotherapy, but which I have found helpful in understanding and working with people.

Assagioli, R. *Psychosynthesis*. (Paperback) New York: The Viking Press, 1971.

Theory and a practical, working method-including several approaches to personal growth such as meditation, encounter group exercises, and inner-imagery. The methods center around the idea that the self, at the heart of each person, can direct the development of the entire personality.

Bachrach, A.J. *Psychological research: an introduction*. (Paperback) New York: Random House, Inc., 1964.

Very good, brief, readable introduction to psychological research. Informally deals with many important considerations in doing and evaluating research in psychology. Many amusing anecdotes and interesting examples.

Barton, A. *Three worlds of therapy: an existential-phenomenological study of the therapies of Freud, Jung, and Rogers.* (Paperback) Palo Alto, Calif.: National Press Books, 1974.

Clear introduction to therapy as practiced by Freud, Jung, and Rogers. Each approach is presented in a three-chapter section including: the view of the patient, the general course of therapy, and taking the same patient through each therapy. Stimulating presentation.

Becker, E. *The denial of death.* New York: The Free Press, 1973. (In paperback, Free Press, 1975).

Becker, a cultural anthropologist, integrates ideas from philosophy, psychology and other areas. Shows great insight into and challenges the theories of such people as Freud, Rank, Kierkegaard, and Jung. An interesting effort to create a meaningful "science of man." Deals with heroism and with man's fears of both life and death. A very gutsy book on the human condition.

Bergmann, G. *Philosophy of science.* Madison, Milwaukee, and London: The University of Wisconsin Press, 1966.

A brief (171 pages), but challenging, heavy theoretical book exploring the philosophy of science as it relates to psychology (the science of behavior). Difficult to understand without some background in philosophy and the sciences.

Colby, K.M. *A primer for psychotherapists.* New York: The Ronald Press Company, 1951.

A very good, basic book of elementary principles of psychotherapy. Colby discusses the aim of psychotherapy; basic theory; the patient; the therapist; behavior during the session; beginning, the middle course of therapy, ending the therapy; and other topics. Interesting presentation of an essentially psychoanalytic and insight orientation to therapy, with good case study material along the way.

Dennison, G. *The lives of children.* (Paperback) New York: Random House, 1969.

A beautifully written, sensitive, intimate journal of a teacher in a small private school on New York's Lower East Side. Dennison became very immersed in the total lives of the children, both in and outside of school. His insights and philosophy of working with children are inspiring and realistic. People who are involved with children can identify with and learn alot from this book.

Dostoevsky, F. *Notes from underground.* (Paperback) New York: E.P. Dutton and Co., Inc.,1960.

An excellent example of how literature can provide great insights into personality. In this work, Dostoevsky presents a deep, understanding view of suffering, depression, and humanity.

Duncan, D.D. *Picasso's Picassos.* New York: Harper and Row, Publishers, 1961.

A very exciting art book. Excellent reproductions from Picasso's private collection of his own work, including paintings from every stage of his artistic development. Intimate, personal text about the artist's life and work. I was particularly impressed with Picasso's tremendous creative energy and courageous experimentation.

Freud, S. *A general introduction to psychoanalysis*. (Paperback) New York: Washington Square Press, 1960.

Twenty eight lectures to laymen which explain the fundamental theories upon which psychoanalysis is based. A thorough explanation, written in clear, understandable language (unlike some other authors who present Freud's ideas in a far more incomprehensible way).

Hall, C. S. and Lindzey, G. *Theories of personality*. New York: John Wiley and Sons,Inc.,1957.

Scholarly, comprehensive, readable overview of major theories of personality. The book includes intelligent comparisons and evaluations of the various theories.

Harper, R.A. *Psychoanalysis and psychotherapy: 36 systems*. (Paperback) Englewood Cliffs, N.J.: Prentice-Hall, Inc., 1959.

Clear, brief understandable presentation of a number of the major approaches to therapy. Nice, basic overview.

Herbert, R.L., ed., *Modern artists on art: Ten unabridged essays*. (Paperback) Englewood Cliffs, New Jersey: Prentice-Hall, Inc., 1964.

Leading innovators in painting and sculpture (e.g. Klee, Kandinsky, Moore) express forcefully and with individuality their views on artistic creation. Many challenging, substantive thoughts relating to ones philosophy of living.

Hergenhahn, B. R. *An introduction to theories of*

learning. Englewood Cliffs, N.J.: Prentice-Hall, Inc., 1976.

Good introductory book on theories of learning. It defines learning, shows how the learning process is studied, views theories of learning in historical perspective, introduces the reader to essential points of major learning theories, and points out some practical implications.

Holt, J. *How children fail.* New York: Pitman Publishing Corporation, 1964. (In Paperback, New York: Dell Publishing Co. Inc., 1970.)

Insightful, straight-forward, exciting book relating to children, psychology, and the philosophies and practices of education. Holt has a wonderful understanding of and sensitivity toward children. He is a keen observer and a fine writer. I found this book to be helpful in relating to both children and their parents in therapy.

Jung, C.G. *Memories, dreams, reflections.* (Paperback) New York: Vintage Books, 1961.

An unusually candid autobiography, written when Jung was eighty two years old. Rather than emphasizing objective events, he stresses his inner life and subjective experiences.

Kaufmann, W., ed., *Existentialism from Dostoevsky to sartre.* (Paperback) New York: Meridian Books, Inc., 1956.

Very good overview of existential philosophy and its implications. Introduces and clearly explains the major existentialists. This book presents relevant and challenging ideas to people in our times.

Laing, R.D. *The politics of experience*. (Paperback) New York: Ballantine Books, Inc., 1968.

One of Laing's most exciting books. An attack on present day assumptions about "normality", arguing that mental sickness is very much a part of our society. He writes personally and powerfully about people, experience, the mystification of experience, and the schizophrenic experience.

Maslow, A.H. *Toward a psychology of being*. (Second Edition) (Paperback) New York: D. Van Nostrand Company, 1968.

Beautifully written, humanistic book. Maslow presents many interesting points relating to growth, motivation, creativity, and values. The book encourages an appreciation and respect for the uniqueness of each individual person.

May, R., ed., *Existential psychology*. (Second Edition) (Paperback) New York: Random House, Inc., 1968.

A short book with chapters by May, Maslow, Feifel, Rogers, and Allport dealing with existential-phenomenological contributions to psychology and psychotherapy. A lucid introduction to the area.

May, R. *The courage to create*. New York: W.W. Norton and Co., Inc., 1975. (In paperback, New York: Bantam Books, Inc., 1976).

Interesting little book on the nature of creativity and creative courage.

Neill, A.S. *Summerhill: A radical approach to child rearing*. (Paperback) New York: Hart Publishing Co., 1964.

Neill candidly discusses his philosophy of child rearing, parenthood, and education. He explains the practices at Summerhill, his private school in England, which stresses freedom and self-regulation for children. Many interesting anecdotes and unique ideas regarding children. A fascinating book to react to-whether you agree or disagree with Neill.

O'Neill, E.G. *Long days journey into night.* New Haven: Yale University Press, 1956.

O'Neill's powerful play about his family. Shows unusual understanding and sensitivity toward the individual personalities-strengths, weaknesses, defenses-and ways they related to one another.

Perls, F.S. *Gestalt therapy verbatim.* Moab, Utah: Real People Press, 1969. (In paperback, Bantam Books, 1971).

Very down-to-earth, readable, practical book on the basic theory and practice of Gestalt Therapy. Stresses the importance of awareness, total self-acceptance, and taking responsibility for all parts of oneself. Presents a number of interesting procedures that I've found to be very valuable in working with people.

Pirsig, R.M. *Zen and the art of motorcycle maintenance.* New York: William Morrow and Company, Inc., 1974. (In paperback, New York: Bantam Books, 1975).

Excellent, non-fiction account of a man's search for truth and himself. An inquiry into values. Interesting focus, comparing classical understanding (underlying form) and romantic understanding (immediate appearance, feelings, impressions). Exciting, inspiring book.

Prather, H. *Notes to myself*. (Paperback) Moab, Utah: Real People Press, 1970.

A collection of sentences and paragraphs relating to Prather's "struggle to become a person." Supports the idea that often what is the most personal and specific is also the most general. A very honest book with which one can easily identify.

Ram Dass. *The only dance there is*. (Paperback) New York: Anchor Books, 1974.

Free flowing book relating to understanding the nature of consciousness. Based on his early training and work as a psychologist (Richard Alpert at the time) prior to studying with his guru in India, and his views following this experience. Presents a variety of ideas from Eastern thought which relate to understanding behavior and the process of therapy.

Redd, W.H., Porterfield, A.L., and Anderson, B.L. *Behavior modification: Behavioral approaches to human problems*. New York: Random House, Inc., 1979.

A very good, thorough book on the theory and practice of behavior modification, and on the behavioral learning research on which it is based. Clear presentation of the various procedures, relevant research, case studies, and personal statements from leaders in the field.

Rogers, C.R. *On becoming a person*. (Paperback) Boston: Houghton-Mifflin, 1961.

A beautiful, warm, human, readable collection of writings summarizing Rogers' years of experience as a therapist. Presents stimulating ideas about healthy human functioning, attitudes and values of the therapist, and things that often help a person to change and grow.

Sidman, M. *Tactics of scientific research.* New York: Basic Books, Inc., Publishers, 1960.

One of the best introductions to understanding and doing research in psychology. Clear, convincing explanations of procedures, and means for evaluating scientific research.

Singer, E. *Key concepts in psychotherapy.* New York: Random House, Inc., 1965.

A scholarly, thought-provoking, informative book which explores the historical development of important concepts relating to the process of psychotherapy. Singer draws upon findings from a variety of areas of psychological research, and presents a contemporary framework for therapy.

Skinner, B.F. *Science and human behavior.* New York: The MacMillan Company, 1953.

Shows the relevance of scientific methodology to understanding and dealing with important aspects of human behavior. Skinner discusses the relationship of scientific findings to such areas as psychotherapy, government, religion, economics, and education. A very convincing book.

Steichen, E., ed., *The family of man.* New York: Maco Magazine Corporation (for The Museum of Modern Art), 1955. (In paperback, New York: A Cardinal Giant, 1955).

As advertised, probably the greatest photographic exhibition of all time. Incredible photographs presented with excerpts from literature. Encouraged my interest (and I'm sure the interest of many others) in photography. Artistic, compassionate, realistic.

Stein, M.I., ed., *Contemporary psychotherapies*. New York: The Free Press of Glencoe, 1961.

Thoughtful presentations of Adlerian, Client-Centered, Existential, Interactional, Interpersonal, Psychoanalytic, Reparative-Adaptational and Transactional orientations to psychotherapy. Ten known therapists present their approaches, and discuss significant issues in the therapeutic process.

Stevens, B. *Don't push the river*. (Paperback) Moah, Utah: Real People Press, 1970.

Down-to-earth, first person account of Steven's use of Gestalt Therapy, Zen, Krishnamurti, and the ways of the American Indian to expand herself and work on personal difficulties. Insightful, honest, engaging book.

Szasz, T.S. *The myth of mental illness*. (Paperback) New York: Dell Publishing Co., Inc., 1961.

A convincing book which discusses a theory of "human conduct" in which mental illness does not exist in the sense that physical diseases exist. People are considered to be responsible for their behavior. A novel, courageous, controversial approach to the study of human behavior and psychotherapy.

Thoreau, H.D. *Walden*. New York: The Modern Library, 1950.

Still one of my favorite books to put things in perspective. His emphases on honest, simple, natural, aware, unpretentious, self-regulated existence are inspiring and timeless.

Wachtel, P.L. *Psychoanalysis and behavior therapy.* New York: Basic Books, Inc. 1977.

This book challenges the assumption that psychodynamic and behavioral approaches to psychotherapy and personality are irreconcilable. With an understanding and respect for both views, he breaks down stereotypes and suggests an integrated model of therapy.

Watts, A.W. *Psychotherapy east and west.* New York: Pantheon Books, 1961. (In paperback; New York: Ballantine Books, Inc., 1969).

Explores how people trap themselves, avoiding dealing with death and lonliness, and compares "ways of liberation" from Eastern and Western thought. Deals with some areas rarely discussed in American books on psychotherapy.